Women and Nation-Building

Cheryl Benard, Seth G. Jones,
Olga Oliker, Cathryn Quantic Thurston,
Brooke K. Stearns, Kristen Cordell

CENTER FOR MIDDLE EAST PUBLIC POLICY

The research described in this report was sponsored by the Government of Qatar and was conducted under the auspices of the Center for Middle East Public Policy within the RAND National Security Research Division (NSRD). NSRD conducts research and analysis for the Office of the Secretary of Defense, the Joint Staff, the Unified Commands, the defense agencies, the Department of the Navy, the Marine Corps, the U.S. Coast Guard, the U.S. Intelligence Community, allied foreign governments, and foundations.

Library of Congress Cataloging-in-Publication Data

Women and nation building / Cheryl Benard ... [et al.].
   p. cm.
   Includes bibliographical references.
   ISBN 978-0-8330-4311-5 (pbk. : alk. paper)
   1. Women in development—Afghanistan. 2. Nation-building—Afghanistan.
3. Women—Afghanistan—Economic conditions. 4. Women—Government policy.
I. Benard, Cheryl, 1953–

HQ1240.5.A34W66 2008
226.30071'5—dc22

2007044221

Cover Photo courtesy of AP Photo/Ed Wray, Photographer

Police recruit Anis Gul, left, and Capt. Gul Jan, right, pose for a picture after Anis Gul signed up for police training Monday, Feb. 16, 2004 in Kabul, Afghanistan. Seven widowed Afghan women signed up for police training, which is being run by the U.S.

The RAND Corporation is a nonprofit research organization providing objective analysis and effective solutions that address the challenges facing the public and private sectors around the world. RAND's publications do not necessarily reflect the opinions of its research clients and sponsors.

RAND® is a registered trademark.

Published 2008 by the RAND Corporation
1776 Main Street, P.O. Box 2138, Santa Monica, CA 90407-2138
1200 South Hayes Street, Arlington, VA 22202-5050
4570 Fifth Avenue, Suite 600, Pittsburgh, PA 15213-2665
RAND URL: http://www.rand.org/
To order RAND documents or to obtain additional information, contact
Distribution Services: Telephone: (310) 451-7002;
Fax: (310) 451-6915; Email: order@rand.org

Preface

This monograph presents the findings of the RAND Corporation's Women and Nation Building Project, which is designed to assess the multilayered development of women's diverse roles in the post-conflict context. The principal task of this study was an overarching consideration of women and nation-building, an exceedingly complex task which was simplified by our ability to use examples from the recent nation-building activities in Afghanistan. Those examples provided several pragmatic points for consideration. Our findings should prove useful and interesting to policymakers, practitioners, and scholars concerned with both the academic and the pragmatic implementation of a more-engendered approach to nation-building. Comments from readers are welcome and can be addressed to the lead author or the center directors listed below.

This research was conducted within the Initiative for Middle Eastern Youth and the RAND Center for Middle East Public Policy. The Initiative for Middle Eastern Youth is funded by donations from private individuals and sources in the State of Qatar. The RAND Center for Middle East Public Policy, part of International Programs at the RAND Corporation, aims to improve public policy by providing decisionmakers and the public with rigorous, objective research on critical policy issues affecting the Middle East.

For more information on the RAND Center for Middle East Public Policy, contact the Director, David Aaron. He can be reached by email at David_Aaron@rand.org; by phone at 310-393-0411, extension 7782; or by mail at RAND, 1776 Main Street, Santa Monica,

California 90407-2138. More information about RAND is available at www.rand.org.

For more information on the Initiative for Middle Eastern Youth, please contact the Director, Cheryl Benard. She can be reached by email at Cheryl_Benard@rand.org; by phone at 703-413-1100, extension 5379; or by mail at RAND, 1200 South Hayes Street, Arlington, Virginia 22202-5050.

Contents

Figures

Tables

Summary

The challenge of nation-building, i.e., dealing with the societal and political aftermaths of conflicts and putting new governments and new social compacts into place, has occupied much international energy during the past several decades. As an art, a process, and a set of competencies, it is still very much in an ongoing learning and experimentation phase. The RAND Corporation has contributed to the emerging knowledge base in this domain through a series of studies that have looked at nation-building enterprises led by the United States and others that were led by the United Nations and have examined the experiences gained during the reconstruction of specific sectors. Our study focuses on gender and nation-building. It considers this issue from two aspects: First, it examines gender-specific impacts of conflict and post-conflict and the ways in which events in these contexts may affect women differently than they affect men. Second, it analyzes the role of women in the nation-building process, in terms of both actual current practices, as far as these could be measured and ascertained, and possible outcomes that might occur if these practices were to be modified.

The study team first surveyed the broader literature on women in development, women and governance, women and conflict, and women in nation-building. It then focused on the case of Afghanistan. This case study was chosen for three reasons: First, it is contemporary, and it offers a longer nation-building "track record" and thus more data than does Iraq, the other contemporary case. Second, the relevant debate and decision line is easy to track because gender issues have been overtly on the table from the beginning of U.S. post-conflict involvement in Afghanistan, in part because of the Taliban's equally overt prior emphasis on gender issues as a defining quality of its regime. Third, in contrast to earlier cases of nation-building, the issue of women's inclusion is presently an official part of any development agenda, so that all the active agents in the nation-building enterprise have made conscious choices and decisions in that regard which can be reviewed and their underlying logic evaluated.

The study concludes with a broad set of analytic and policy recommendations. First, we identify the gaps in data collection and provide specific suggestions for improvement. Then, we recommend three shifts in emphasis that we believe are likely to strengthen the prospects of stability and enhance the outcomes of nation-building programs: a more genuine emphasis on the broader concept of human security from the earliest phases of the nation-building effort; a focus on establishing governance based on principles of equity and consistent rule of law from the start; and economic inclusion of women in the earliest stages of reconstruction activities.

Acknowledgments

The authors wish to thank those individuals and organizations whose assistance made this study possible. First of all, we thank the government of Qatar, which provided the funding for the research through a grant to RAND's Initiative for Middle Eastern Youth (IMEY).

We would also like to thank Karla Cunningham, Daniel Byman, and Ambassador James Dobbins for their careful reviews of this manuscript.

A number of the National Solidarity Program's facilitating partners provided data and comments drawn from their fieldwork in Afghanistan: the Agency for Technical Cooperation and Development (ACTED), the Afghan Development Agency (ADA), Afghan Aid (AAD), the Cooperative for American Remittances to Europe (CARE), Coordination of Humanitarian Assistance (CHA), Concern, the Danish Committee for Aid to Afghan Refugees (DACAAR), German Agro-Action (GAA), the Ghazni Rural Support Program (GRSP), the Oxford Committee for Famine Relief (Oxfam), Ockenden International (OI), Relief International (RI), the Swedish Committee for Afghanistan (SCA), Sanayee Development Foundation (SDF), Solidarités (Aide Humanitaire d'Urgence), and the United Nations Human Settlement Program (UN-HABITAT).

Acronyms and Abbreviations

AA	Action Aid
AAD	Afghan Aid
ACSF	Afghan Civil Society Forum
ACTED	Agency for Technical Cooperation and Development
ADA	Afghan Development Agency
AKDN	Aga Khan Development Network
ANA	Afghan National Army
ANBP	Afghanistan New Beginnings Programme
AREU	Afghanistan Research and Evaluation Unit
AWEC	Afghan Women's Education Centre
AWRC	Afghan Women's Resource Centre
BRAC	Bangladesh Rural Advancement Committee
CARE	Cooperative for American Remittances to Europe
CDC	Community Development Council
CDP	community development plan
CHA	Coordination of Humanitarian Assistance
CSO	Central Statistical Office
DACAAR	Danish Committee for Aid to Afghan Refugees
DHS	Demographic and Health Surveys

DPT	diphtheria, pertussis, and tetanus
EDI	Education Development Index
EFA	Education for All
EMIS	Education Management Information System
FP	facilitating partner
GAA	German Agro-Action
GDI	Gender Development Index
GEEI	Gender Equality in Education Index
GEI	Global Education Initiative
GEM	Gender Empowerment Measure
GMR	Global Monitoring Report
GNP	Gross National Product
GRSP	Ghazni Rural Support Program
HDI	Human Development Index
HTAC	Help the Afghan Children
IAS	Institute for Afghan Studies
ICRC	International Committee of the Red Cross
ICSED	International Standard Classification of Education
IED	improvised explosive device
INL	Bureau of International Narcotics and Law Enforcement Affairs
IO	international organization
IRC	International Rescue Committee
ISAF	International Security Assistance Force
JEMB	Joint Electoral Management Body
JEMBS	Joint Electoral Management Body Secretariat
MADERA	Mission d'Aide au Développement des Economies Rurales

MDG	Millenium Development Goals
NGO	non-governmental organization
MID	Militarized Interstate Dispute
MOWA	Ministry of Women's Affairs
MRRD	Ministry for Rural Rehabilation and Development
NPO/RRA	Norwegian Project Office/Rural Rehabilitation Association
NSP	National Solidarity Program
OECD	Organization for Economic Cooperation and Development
OI	Ockenden International
ONHCR	Office of the High Commissioner for Refugees
Oxfam	Oxford Committee for Famine Relief
PIN	People in Need
PRT	Provincial Reconstruction Team
RAWA	Revolutionary Association of the Women of Afghanistan
RI	Relief International
RPG	rocket-propelled grenade
SCA	Swedish Committee for Afghanistan
S/CRS	U.S. State Department Office of the Coordinator for Reconstruction and Stabilization
SDF	Sanayee Development Foundation
SO	social organizer
UNDP	United Nations Development Programme
UNESCO	United Nations Educational, Scientific and Cultural Organization
UNFPA	United Nations Fund for Population Activities
UN-HABITAT	United Nations Human Settlement Program

UNICEF	United Nations Children's Fund
UNIFEM	United Nations Development Fund for Women
USAID	United States Agency for International Development
WAPHA	Women's Alliance for Peace and Human Rights in Afghanistan
WAW	Women for Afghan Women
WFP	World Food Programme
WHO	World Health Organization
WLUML	Women Living Under Muslim Laws
ZOA	Zuid Oost Azie Refugee Care

CHAPTER ONE

Introduction

This study was undertaken to examine the role of women in post-conflict nation-building and, conversely, to better understand the impact of post-conflict societal circumstances and nation-building processes on the status and situation of female populations.

Like research on post-conflict nation-building in general, our work was hampered by the lack of availability and poor reliability of data. One of our principal recommendations, therefore, concerns improving data collection. Without reliable data, the efficacy of programs is very difficult to assess, and this presents a serious obstacle to the development of effective programs and instruments of nation-building.

Fortunately, the case study of Afghanistan offered sufficient substantive information to allow for preliminary conclusions on a number of levels and for several reconstruction sectors. By embedding the available country-specific information in the broader data provided by empirical studies of the relationship between gender regimes[1] and governance, domestic stability, socioeconomic development, conduct of regional foreign-policy relations, bellicosity, and corruption—all of which are pivotal components of the process and outcome of nation-building—we have been able to derive at least some preliminary markers on this evolving topic.

Our findings indicate that greater stability and improved outcomes would likely result from a shift in the usual emphasis of nation-building. This shift involves three elements: First, security must be

---

[1] In this monograph, we use the term *gender regime* to mean the dominant societal arrangement between men and women regarding rights, power, and status.

understood and implemented more consistently with the concept of human security. Second, governance should be placed on a foundation of equity and consistent rule of law from the start of the nation-building process. Third, women must be included even in the earliest phases of economic reconstruction and administrative reconstitution.

In the immediate post-conflict environment, the goal of preventing renewed violence often overshadows everything else, because failure to do so could imperil everything else. This can lead to tensions between civil-society actors, including advocates of women's interests, and the architects and implementers of the nation-building effort. These tensions result from the conflict between a moral sentiment on one side and a pragmatic assumption on the other. Nation-building and the prevention of renewed conflict, however, are arguably too complex and too important to be conducted on the basis of either sentiment or assumptions.

Moral sentiment argues that a post-conflict society must respect the human rights of women, even if that respect comes at a cost. Implementers often argue for a gradual and cautious approach, contending that too bold a stance on issues of gender will imperil the entire program and, with it, the fragile new peace. While we found the data on women and nation-building to be limited in general, data showing a correlation between a policy of gender equity and destabilization are nonexistent. At best, we were able to find anecdotal suppositions linking fundamentalist opposition to the Soviet occupation of Afghanistan with the Soviets' association with emancipatory values. Does a policy of support for values of equality, for women's economic and political inclusion, and for social justice carry an elevated risk of political destabilization and return to conflict? If it does, evidence of such a risk has yet to be presented. Any policy operating on that assumption—which has far-reaching consequences—must be evidence-based, or it can be considered only as highly irresponsible. In fact, the available empirical evidence points to an opposite conclusion: that societies placed on the path of equity and the rule of law are more peaceful and more prosperous, and the status of women is not merely a litmus test, but also an active agent in bringing about such an outcome.

A significant body of literature specifically addresses the issue of women in regard to conflict and nation-building. Much of that literature is declamatory rather than analytic, originating with advocacy groups and consisting of assertions of the importance of gender and women's inclusion and the potential beneficial role of women and—as the writers presume—their "different" voice and values as a pacifying force in international relations. However, there are important exceptions, as will be seen.

There is nothing wrong with moral argumentation, and many of the important advances of the last century on the gender front were achieved in large part due to such arguments. The problem is that a moral argument can be interpreted to mean that pragmatic reasons would argue against the desired course of action. And indeed, we can find that very assumption represented among nation-builders, sometimes tacitly, sometimes overtly. In a recent article in *Foreign Affairs*, Ambassador Swanee Hunt describes the response she received from a colonel at the Pentagon shortly after the United States' "shock and awe" attack on Iraq in 2003: "When I urged him to broaden his search for the future leaders of Iraq, which had yielded hundreds of men and only seven women, he responded, 'Ambassador Hunt, we'll address women's issues after we get the place secure.'"[2]

Overview of Nation-Building

Few policymakers responsible for nation-building would argue against the ultimate goal of establishing equitable, democratic, and egalitarian societies in which the human rights of women are respected. Many, however, express the fear that pursuing that goal "too soon" may rock the boat, and that in dealing with a boat so shaky that it may capsize anyway, you just can't take the risk.

First, they may argue, you have to stabilize the situation, obtain the buy-in of important stakeholders, and take care of the former combatants. As you gradually lay the groundwork for a peaceful civil soci-

---

[2] Hunt, 2007.

ety and a democracy, you are preparing the way for improvements in the status and rights of women, which will, it is to be hoped, grow over time.

It is impracticable to field-test this premise, to separate nation-building cases into two parallel scenarios, one in which women are fully included in the peace talks and the nation-building effort from the start and another in which they are marginalized, with other circumstances being largely comparable.

Fortunately, a large and growing body of empirical work addresses the component parts of stabilization and nation-building, enabling us to extrapolate with some confidence. Nation-building requires that the prior armed conflict come to a halt, with the former combatants agreeing to pursue their respective agendas through the legitimate political process instead of through violence. It requires the establishment of a system of governance, including the ability to maintain order, guarantee the fulfillment of international obligations and human rights, and deliver essential social services. Violence and arbitrary exercises of power must be replaced by the rule of law and due process. In stratified or divided societies, the various parties must achieve a social compact regulating their status and relations. The society itself must be viable or be plausibly seen as moving toward viability in terms of its economy and its political process. Finally, its relationship with its neighbors and with the international community must be settled and made subordinate to peaceful and legal processes in place of violence and war. One need not look far to see examples of instability leaking across borders—in the form of refugees, diseases, drought, and crime—causing the primary and growing efforts at reform to fail.[3]

Empirical findings are available for each of the essential components of nation-building. They contain a great deal of information about the role of gender in these processes, even where that issue is not part of the original study design. These studies indicate the following:

- The conduct of states in their foreign relations tends to mirror their domestic conduct. If the political culture of a country shows

---

[3] Carment, et al., 2006. For more on the data, see the Country Indicators for Foreign Policy Project web site, Carleton University, http://www.carleton.ca/cifp/about.htm.

a propensity toward violence and disregard of the rights of weaker strata of its society, that country will be likely to initiate violence when disputes occur with its neighbors.

- The "demographic shift," which generally represents the transition to modernity, involves such conditions as smaller family size, higher longevity, increased maternal and infant survival rates, greater societal prosperity, and increased political stability. These go along with increased gender equality.
- Economic development is strongly elevated when women enter the marketplace. Women's economic participation raises development, not only by decreasing the dependency ratio and increasing the proportion of wage earners to dependents who must be supported, but also because women have been found to be significantly more likely to reinvest their earnings in things that benefit the family than men are.
- In many settings, including women in the labor force has proven to be the one step that lifts families out of the cycle of poverty.[4]
- The presence of women in institutions such as the police and administrative bureaucracies is associated with decreases in corruption.[5]

These findings, combined with the observations from our Afghanistan case study, incline us to argue for an earlier rather than a later emphasis on the values known to be associated with stable democratic societies governed by the rule of law. Among these, gender equity and women's inclusion play a central role.

At the heart of this issue lies a question that, although it goes beyond the scope of the present study, should concern anyone interested in nation-building. The question pertains to the timing, cost, methodology, and mix of the assorted international actions associated with nation-building: military interventions to end the conflict, stability operations, peacekeeping operations, state-building, and "nation-building proper." Namely, is it better to aim for a rapid, minimally

---

[4] King and Mason, 2001; Coleman, 2004a.

[5] Dollar, Fismond, and Gatti, 1999.

costly end to a conflict and then to cobble together a quick interim government with many obvious flaws, on the assumption that a gradual return to normalcy will allow for the gradual growth of civil society, crowding out the negative participants and forces? Is it more effective to allow a repressive social order to become reentrenched and then work to effect a reversal? Or is better to push for an optimized outcome, accepting the higher risk and up-front human costs that are likely to result?

In Afghanistan, for example, might the outcome have been different if the coalition had chosen to defeat the Taliban with its own ground troops instead of using its Northern Alliance surrogates, to then maintain a much larger International Security Assistance Force (ISAF), and to oversee and administer the rebuilding of an Afghan state for five or ten years? Would the probably greater loss of life at the outset have exceeded the smaller but steady loss of life resulting from the prolonged conflict period or a more costly peace-building operation? The issue of how best to rebuild a nation begs further review, as the consequences of that choice are potentially grave.

It would be useful to devise metrics or to design a study that compares the costs of an earlier, more-difficult stabilization effort bent on establishing a government based on equity, merit, and the rule of law with those of a quicker stabilization effort that emplaced a government that appeased and included former warlords and other negative stakeholders.

Might the potential positive effects of women's participation—lower corruption rates, faster economic growth, and improved overall standards of living—make a difference to the post-conflict trajectories of very volatile societies? We don't know, but given the troubled recoveries we are seeing in places that have been applying the more conventional approach—including Afghanistan and Iraq—one might at some point wish to attempt the experiment.

If a new government is to achieve legitimacy and obtain popular support, it must deliver tangible improvements in the quality of people's lives within a reasonable period of time. In Afghanistan, we are beginning to see what happens when such tangible improvements fail to materialize. Support for the Karzai government is beginning to fray, as people question its ability to affect their lives positively and to deliver on its promises. They see the same former stakeholders again rising to prominence, and they see corruption and arbitrary decisions instead of the rule of law.[6]

While it is likely true that a society will not go from crass inequity to perfect justice within the space of a few years, a plausible and fundamental direction of intent is important. In the grand scheme of things, the items that were looted by rampaging Iraqis in the hours and days following the fall of Baghdad did not matter, and the decision to let the looting go on during this chaotic interim period did not seem monumental. But in retrospect, many now see this as a tragic turning point. Tolerating the looting sent the message that the coalition was not there to install the rule of law and that its troops were either not willing or not able to impose order and good governance.

Similarly, in the grand scheme of things, it perhaps "does not matter" if several dozen young women burn themselves to death in Herat every year because there is no legal recourse for them when they are subjected to abuse. However, tolerating a situation in which existing laws are not enforced and victims are left unprotected may send a larger negative message, leading civil society to conclude that the new order is either unwilling or unable to enforce its purported laws and values.[7] And when the international community responds to the immolation deaths not through a forceful police and judicial program, but by opening a burn unit in the city of Herat, this is a message too, informing civil society that it can hope for charity but not for justice. Neither of those messages is likely to bolster the nation-building effort in that country.

Women and Nation-Building

The primary goal of any immediate post-conflict period is to prevent the renewed outbreak of violence and to set the foundation for a stable

---

[6] See, for example, Bergen (2007).

[7] World Bank, 2005; Amnesty International, 2005a.

society with a lowered propensity for war. As stated in the RAND study *A Beginner's Guide to Nation-Building*, "the prime objective of nation-building is to leave behind a society at peace with itself and its neighbors."[8]

Such societies have been found to share certain characteristics. Conversely, researchers have developed metrics for identifying "failed and fragile states." The purpose of one such study was to identify the interventions most likely to bolster fragile states and prevent them from sliding into conflict, in order to more effectively target Canadian aid programs.[9] The project did not initially foresee a gender dimension. However, once the data were compiled, gender emerged as a particularly relevant factor:

> The fact that strong performance on gender measurements correlates closely with stability may come as a surprise to some. . . . To a certain extent, the correlation between gender development and stability mirrors the relationship between development and stability; indeed, the 2003 GDI [Gender Development Index] correlates with HDI [Human Development Index] at over 0.99%, suggesting the two indices actually capture virtually identical performance measures. . . . Nonetheless [our study] suggests a strong correlation to stability that goes beyond raw measures of development.[10]

In other words, it was not simply a matter of more-developed societies being more stable and coincidentally characterized by certain advanced societal features, including greater gender equity. Rather, the findings pointed to the conclusion that "gender parity may . . .

---

[8] Dobbins et al., 2007, p. xxiv.

[9] The project reviewed more than 70 indicators related to the authority, legitimacy, and capacity of states, organizing them into "cluster areas," including governance, economics, security and crime, human development, demographics, and environment. To take economic and other fluctuations into account, five-year averages were used. On the basis of these datasets, a score was calculated for each country, and countries were grouped into four risk and stability categories. See Carment et al. (2006). Also data at Country Indicators for Foreign Policy Project, Carleton Univeristy, web site, http://www.carleton.ca/cifp/about.htm.

[10] Carment et al., 2006, p. 22.

play a strong and measurable role in the stability of the state," even when separated from another known correlation, that between general societal-development levels and stability.

By contrast, a similar correlation was not found between democracy and stability. Full autocracies and full democracies tended to be the most stable; transitional and partial democracies were more likely to be volatile. Nation-builders who push with determination for the installation of new democracies but are cautious on issues related to the status of women thus may be approaching matters in the wrong order—at least if stability is their principal aim.

Other work with special relevance to the issue of women and nation-building has examined the relationship between external bellicosity and domestic gender equality.[11] Not illogically, it appears that the "political culture" of a state is reflected in both its domestic and its international behavior. Thus, countries with repressive, hierarchically stratified social orders are more inclined to show a proclivity toward violence and oppression in their foreign policy: "State domestic culture in both its behavior and underlying values helps predict state international behavior during interstate disputes and crises."[12]

The World Bank in 2003 supported a study to test this relationship by examining the 141 states represented in the Militarized Interstate Dispute (MID) database. It found a robust correlation between domestic gender inequality and external aggression, leading the author to conclude that "gender equality is not merely a matter of social justice but of international security in predicting state aggressiveness internationally."[13]

---

[11] Caprioli, 2003.

[12] Ibid., p. 196. The study builds on a significant body of earlier work, including Rummel (1997), which found violence to be significantly more likely "when political power is centralized, non-democratic, and highly dependent upon one's social group membership, be it race, religion, ethnicity, or some cultural division (gender)" (cited in Caprioli, 2003, p. 200).

[13] The project design controlled for other variables that were likely to be relevant and/or to distort the results, such as the number of alliance partners (states with more alliance partners are less likely to choose first use of force) (Caprioli, 2003, p. 209).

Women and Nation-Building: The Lessons of Afghanistan

Does an overt effort to emplace the values of gender equity rock the boat and imperil a fragile peace? This fear has been especially pronounced with regard to Afghanistan, which is believed to have a history of rebelling against liberators, both foreign and domestic, when the liberation effort extends to its women. The present nation-building exercise in Afghanistan offers at least two major examples of an overt enfranchisement and inclusion effort and allows us to review the premise: the inclusion of women in the Afghan political process (in the drafting of the constitution and the formal enshrining of their equal rights and a high percentage of representation in parliament, in the Loya Jirgas (tribal grand councils), as voters, as candidates, as ministers) and as beneficiaries and actors within the National Solidarity Program (NSP), a World Bank–funded program that distributed resources countrywide to communities that met certain prerequisites, including conducting a local census, devising a local development plan, learning to administer funding, and establishing a community council that was required to include women. These efforts are described in subsequent chapters.

In summary, the acceptance of women's political participation by Afghan mainstream society—as reflected in opinion polls, in survey research, and in the actual behavior of the public—was higher than outside observers had anticipated. As we will see, a flexible process in which local conditions and concerns were noted and adapted to[14] contributed to that outcome.

The explicit gender-related goals of the NSP and the visible presence of foreign implementers could have been expected to invoke resistance. A large number of non-governmental organizations (NGOs) were deployed in the field to implement and oversee this program, and their records provide rich material for understanding and assessing the processes on the ground. Their experience shows that while it was not necessarily easy to obtain the women's participation, neither was this

---

[14] For example, it was made widely known that women did not have to be photographed for their voter identity cards, a widespread campaign of voter education was carried out, and segregated voting stations were provided.

in any instance a "deal-breaker" or even a major source of discord. Rather, what was required was an ongoing interactive process in which obstacles and local concerns were continuously met with discourse and new solutions.

There is still inadequate understanding of how conflict may transform a society. A prolonged or severe conflict can often effect substantial changes to the makeup of the population and its culture, even without the additional impact of trauma. The composition of the population may change significantly. Often, countries lose their educated middle class, which is sometimes specifically targeted for eradication; or, having more options, the middle class may be quicker to flee and more reluctant to return. As men join the battle and are killed, women may find themselves increasingly in the role of head of the family, even where that goes against the traditional sexual division of responsibilities. As the infrastructure of a country is degraded, public-health levels may decline precipitously, and if the conflict is protracted, education levels may drop, even to the point where illiteracy returns. Until we have a better understanding of how to measure these changes, we should not assume that what we knew about a society prior to a conflict is still valid after the conflict.

There were indications as early as 2002 that Afghan society had emerged from its prolonged period of conflict and the rule of the Taliban with an elevated interest in progress, an inclination to trust foreign policing more than the baggage-ridden local authority, and a heightened acceptance of a new and expanded public role for women. At the same time, Afghan women have stepped forward to support the post-conflict regime and its new values.

A poll conducted in 2004 by the Asia Foundation found that issues of gender equity were of great concern to Afghan women.[15] Four of the concerns they highlighted overtly related to women's status, and education access, health-care provision, and poverty were also strongly affiliated with gender. During the 2004 presidential election and the 2005 parliamentary elections, women worked as poll monitors, voter educators, and administrators of returns. These tasks were important

---

[15] Asia Foundation, 2004.

both as jobs for women and because they encouraged women to vote by creating a secure environment for them. The women who participated in the voting and stood as candidates faced considerable risk—ordinary women ritually prepared themselves for death before setting out for the polling places.

In the Loya Jirga, women were among the most outspoken opponents of the reinstatement of drug lords and warlords, despite the risks attending such a public posture. In more than one instance, tribal elders from remote, highly conservative provinces first sent a young woman as their envoy to the parliament and later journeyed to the capital in her entourage to support her anti-corruption message.[16] Women have been at the forefront of calls to disarm private militias, organizing protests and signing petitions. Women called for disarmament in the Afghan Women's Bill of Rights, as well as in the Declaration of Afghan Women's NGOs.[17] Women have also played a direct role in the disarmament, demobilization, and reintegration of combatants.[18] And although in small numbers, women have been incorporated into the Afghan police force; 105 women graduates of the police academy are currently working as police officers.[19]

But what about security in the immediate sense? Is there a contradiction between the goal of establishing security—defined narrowly as "avoiding a renewed outbreak of hostilities"—and the goal of establishing a more gender-equitable society? The presently available facts do not point to such a contradiction.

First, opinion polls and surveys underscore the fact that for the Afghan population at large, "security" is intuitively understood as meaning "human security." Clean water, the ability to obtain medical help for injuries and illnesses, safety from crime and intimidation, a chance to obtain at least a minimal living standard, not just the absence of flying bullets, are what people aspire to. And human security, as noted

---

[16] BBC News, 2005a. See Chapter Four for further discussion.

[17] Sultan, 2005, p. 22.

[18] United Nations Development Programme, 2006.

[19] United Nations, WomanWarPeace portal on women, peace and security, http://www.womenwarpeace.org/afghanistan/afghanistan.htm (as of October 25, 2007).

above, is fostered by a certain type of society. If we follow negative human-security indicators back a few steps, the oppression of women is often revealed as a root cause. The failure of infants and children to survive is generally the result of mothers being too young, too ill, and too weak to give birth to and to nurse healthy children, or of themselves not being able to survive childbirth long enough to care for those infants and children.[20] If children under five years of age are dying in large numbers, dysentery, caused by dirty water and poor hygiene, is often a major contributing cause. Where women have access to money and a say in how it is spent, there is a statistically greater likelihood of getting investment in wells and clean water, and a greater likelihood of having mothers who understand basic health care and hygiene. High levels of crime and intimidation tend to be the result of a pervasive entitlement culture, as opposed to a rule-of-law culture. And so on.

But what about the most basic and immediate struggle for security, the battle against a renewed insurgency and terrorist attacks? Must one perhaps scale back one's progressive efforts to avoid agitating conservative populations? Not according to the experiences of U.S. commanders in the field.

Reports from some of Afghanistan's most perilous locales—areas too dangerous for an NGO presence, where Provincial Reconstruction Teams (PRTs) instead attempt to provide some services and create links to the local population—reflect a strong desire on the part of the local population for socioeconomic advancement and improvements in their daily lives.

Health-care operations have been particularly effective in winning local support. On repeated occasions, female patients in health clinics, thankful for care received and motivated to support the new order that provided it, have volunteered valuable tactical information to U.S. forces. In June 2003, a woman informed soldiers on a U.S. firebase in the Bermel Valley about foreign fighters laying landmines.

---

[20] See Save the Children (2007). The report notes that infant and child mortality is highest in countries that have experienced recent conflict; it names Afghanistan, Liberia, and Sierra Leone as the three current worst cases and Iraq as one of the countries with the most pronounced recent decline.

Pursuing her lead, U.S. forces found the ambush team and initiated an attack. The U.S. forces disabled the entire patrol, gathered intelligence about insurgent techniques, and walked away with no casualties—instead of driving into a coordinated IED/RPG (improvised explosive device/rocket-propelled grenade) ambush.[21]

Finally, then, we turn our discussion to a consideration of the priorities of the women themselves. Too often, nation-building missions seek to install a non-indigenous social structure onto the society. Information on Afghanistan's rich historical, social, and familial norms can be derived from listening to its women. Nation-builders should work to weave in traditionally salient practices along with the fabric of a strong nation and the necessity for international human rights.

While far from representative, focus groups we held with middle-school and high-school girls in Kandahar and Kabul in 2004 revealed strong consensus on four issues: They wanted to have a choice in the selection of their future husbands. They wanted to earn an income. They believed that their prospects for happiness were improved enormously by the fall of the Taliban and were insistent that the international presence continue in order for those gains to be safeguarded. The fourth issue was more abstract: Their standing as human beings had been elevated, they said, and they did not want to lose this again. In the words of Sameera, a seventh-grader at Zarghona High School in Kandahar, "If you [the West] leave Afghanistan, Al Qaeda will come again."

The priority of these women is also our priority. It is critical that we try to target and improve the lives of women and girls in post-conflict reconstruction, backing our plans with resources and actions and assessing our failures as well as our successes.

---

[21] U.S. Army Training and Doctrine Command, 2004, p. 19.

CHAPTER TWO

The Security Dimension and Women

Within the post-conflict security context, women participate as victims, combatants, protectors, and peacemakers—all difficult and complex roles that deserve our attention. This chapter seeks to better understand women and security during reconstruction and nation-building missions, highlighting recent examples from Afghanistan. It asks three questions: How has the security environment impacted women in Afghanistan? How have women impacted the security environment there? And how can the security situation be improved for women and for the country more broadly?

In 2001, the United States orchestrated a rapid military victory in Afghanistan. A combination of U.S. Special Operations and CIA forces, air power, and Afghan indigenous forces overthrew the Taliban regime in less than three months, suffering only a dozen U.S. casualties.[1] While fighting continued over the next several years, the United States and other international actors began assisting Afghanistan with reconstruction. Afghan leaders signed the Bonn Agreement on December 5, 2001, which established a timetable for achieving peace and security, reestablishing key government institutions, and reconstructing Afghanistan.

We define *security* broadly to include what is increasingly being referred to as "human security." Human security involves creating political, social, environmental, economic, and cultural systems that together give people the building blocks of survival, livelihood, and

---

[1] On the overthrow of the Taliban regime, see Schroen (2005), Biddle (2002), Berntsen and Pezzullo (2005), Woodward (2002).

dignity. It covers a range of issues, including personal security, political security, community security, economic security, food security, health security, and environmental security.[2] As early as 1945, then–U.S. Secretary of State Edward R. Stettinius identified the two fundamental components of human security and their connections:

> The battle of peace has to be fought on two fronts. The first front is the security front, where victory spells freedom from fear. The second is the economic and social front, where victory means freedom from want. Only victory on both fronts can assure the world of an enduring peace.[3]

This chapter argues that security and women have a double-edged relationship in Afghanistan. First, the security environment has negatively impacted women. A major problem is violence against women. An Amnesty International report concludes:

> Violence against women and girls in Afghanistan is pervasive; few women are exempt from the reality or threat of violence. Afghan women and girls live with the risk of: abduction and rape by armed individuals; forced marriage; being traded for settling disputes and debts; and face daily discrimination from all segments of society as well as by state officials.[4]

Second, women are one of the greatest potential sources of peace and security for Afghanistan, through their participation in humanitarian operations and other efforts. Together, these two cross-cutting effects suggest that long-term peace in Afghanistan is at least partly a function of (1) improving the security environment for women and (2) increasing their positive contributions toward peace. The role of women is frequently underappreciated in the security environment. But women play a critical role in ending 30 years of conflict in Afghanistan.

---

[2] United Nations Development Programme, 1994.

[3] United Nations Development Programme, 2005, p. 12.

[4] Amnesty International, 2005b.

This chapter first outlines the historical context of women and security in Afghanistan. It then examines the impact of the security situation on women and explores the ways in which women are targets of violence. Next, it outlines the positive role that women have played in improving the security situation. Finally, it brings these strands together and recommends steps that can help decrease violence against women and increase their positive contributions.

The Historical Context

Afghan women have historically been the target of efforts both to curtail and to promote their security and rights. Force has been employed to carry out both policies. In 1928, King Amanallah abdicated his throne following a tribal rebellion that in part had formed to oppose such reforms as schooling for girls and restrictions on polygamy. Reforms to promote women's rights were again attempted in the 1960s and 1970s, but their effects were largely limited to women in urban areas of the country. In 1965, the government of Afghanistan submitted a comment to the Commission on the Status of Women, addressing the issue of a United Nations Declaration on Eliminating Discrimination Against Women. It stated that eliminating discrimination required the "combating of traditions, customs, and usages which thwart the advancement of women" and advocated the use of affirmative-action policies to accomplish this.[5]

In 1978, the communist People's Democratic Party of Afghanistan obtained control of the country and attempted to institute radical reforms affecting the rights and status of women. These reforms included the prohibition of a number of cultural practices regarding marriage and family law that were widely considered "Islamic" within Afghan society. In fact, however, some were tribal and traditional customs that were at variance with orthodox Islam. In the summer of 1978, a wave of Afghan refugees fled to Pakistan, partly in response to the government's use of force to implement a policy of compulsory

---

[5] Fraser, 1999, p. 891.

education for women—a policy viewed by some as a source of dishonor to the family.[6] The Soviet invasion of Afghanistan led to the rise of the *mujahidin*, a coalition of Islamist tribal groups that fought to push the Soviets out.

The *mujahidin* rejected the reforms instituted by the communist government and equated a return of women to their traditional roles to a return to the nation's Islamic identity. A restricted role for women became part of their Islamic ideology and Afghan nationalism. Amnesty International described how "women were treated as the spoils of war" by the *mujahidin*:

> Particularly between 1992 and 1995, armed guards have used these (cultural) norms as weapons of war, engaging in rape and sexual assault against women as an ultimate means of dishonoring entire communities and reducing people's capacity to resist military advances.[7]

Further, *mujahidin* factions, including the Northern Alliance, often visibly tried to demonstrate their commitment to Islam and traditional Afghan identity by imposing restrictions on women's freedom of movement, education, access to health care, and employment. However, because the *mujahidin* had an unorganized structure, its enforcement of these restrictions was inconsistent and unsystematic. In Kabul, women continued to work in government departments, education, and health care, although at their own risk.

By the late 1990s, the Taliban had conquered more than two-thirds of Afghanistan. Taliban leaders sought to impose a radical interpretation of Sunni Islam, a version derived from the Deobandi school of thought.[8] Once in motion, such violent rebellion-oriented movements are particularly difficult to stop in nations with low gender equity. A long-standing inequity from gender-separated roles creates the norms of violence that prompt forward momentum and encouragement of

---

[6] Moghadam, 1999, pp. 172–204.

[7] Amnesty International, 1999b.

[8] Roy, 1990; Rashid, 2000; Maley, 2001.

the violence.[9] The Taliban denied women and girls access to secondary, and in many cases, even primary education; adequate health care; and employment (except in limited circumstances). It severely restricted their freedom of movement, freedom of association, and an array of other internationally recognized human rights. The Taliban's Department for the Preservation of Virtue and Prevention of Vice publicly beat and flogged Afghan women and girls for displaying any part of their face or ankles, wearing white socks, traveling without a male family member, being involved in education as a teacher or student, or seeking employment.[10] This was done in the name of protecting women's security and fulfilling the dictates of Islam. In contrast to the *mujahidin*, the Taliban had a strong organizational capacity to enforce these policies, particularly in urban areas. It often did so through beatings and extreme violence.[11]

The Impact of Security on Women

Since the overthrow of the Taliban government, women have been affected by the security environment in several ways. As noted earlier, we define security broadly to include human security, which typically means safety from such chronic threats as hunger and disease and protection from sudden and hurtful disruptions in the patterns of daily life—whether in homes, in jobs, or in communities.[12] The community element is especially important, as feminist perceptions of security draw upon the "political, economic, and ecological" factors of social interactions, considering them just as important as military might, a fact illustrated by the finding that gender-equitable societies are considerably less violent than their inequitable counterparts.[13]

---

[9] Caprioli, 2005.

[10] Sultan, 2005, pp. 3–5.

[11] See, for example, United Nations, 1999.

[12] See, for example, Paris, 2001, pp. 87–102; Khong, 2001; Suhrke, 1999, pp. 265–276; Stoett, 1999; Thomas and Wilkin, 1999.

[13] Caprioli and Boyer, 2001; also see Caprioli, 2003.

The United Nations Commission on Human Security defines human security as protection of "the vital core of all human lives in ways that enhance human freedoms and human fulfillment. Human security means protecting fundamental freedoms—freedoms that are the essence of life. It means protecting people from critical (severe) and pervasive (widespread) threats and situations."[14]

We next examine the impact of five security areas on women: the social and economic front, insurgent attacks, crime, domestic violence, and justice.

The Social and Economic Front

Since 2001, the economic and social security of Afghan women has been directly affected in several ways. A public-opinion poll conducted by the Asia Foundation identified several key problems: education and literacy (cited by 47 percent of the respondents), women's rights (33 percent), health care (32 percent), control by men (21 percent), poverty (18 percent), forced marriages or dowry abuses (17 percent), and lack of permission to leave their homes (12 percent). Figure 2.1 summarizes the survey results.[15] Only 6 percent of men and women referred to "security" in its most conventional definition as a major problem for women.

Insurgent Attacks

Insurgent forces in Afghanistan have conducted a wide variety of attacks against international and Afghan targets, including girls and women. The main insurgent groups are the Taliban, Hezb-i-Islami Gulbuddin, foreign fighters (mostly Arabs and Central Asians), and tribal militias based in Pakistan and Afghanistan. The Taliban, the largest group, have an estimated 2,000 to 5,000 fighters, including a recent influx of new members—sometimes referred to as the "neo-Taliban"—who have been recruited at madrassas and other locations in Afghanistan and

---

[14] United Nations, 2003, p. 4.

[15] Asia Foundation, 2004.

Figure 2.1
Key Problems Affecting Afghan Women

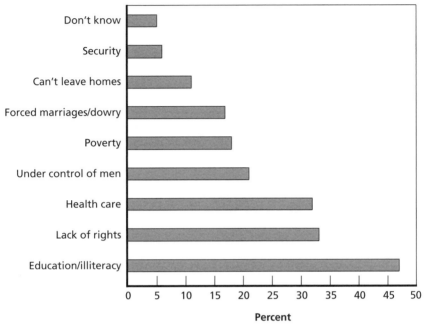

RAND *MG579-2.1*

Pakistan.[16] The Taliban has allied with a number of tribes and figures, including Gulbuddin Hekmatyar and Jalaluddin Haqqani. Armed insurgents have been responsible for assassinations; ambushes and raids using small arms and grenades; shelling with 107-mm and 122-mm rockets and 60-, 82-, and 120-mm mortars; and attacks with IEDs.[17] Major spikes in insurgent-initiated violence have usually been a function of specific campaigns, such as the insurgent attempt to destabilize the October 2004 presidential election and the 2005 parliamentary elections by targeting Afghan and international personnel involved in organizing, registering, and participating in them. Insurgents also conducted a major campaign tied to the U.S. handover to NATO forces

---

[16] Seth G. Jones, interview with U.S. Defense Department officials, Kabul, Afghanistan, September 2006.

[17] United States Marine Corps, 2004; U.S. Army Training and Doctrine Command, 2003.

in the south in the summer and fall of 2006. Attacks have occurred throughout the country, though most have been in the southern and eastern provinces of Helmand, Paktia, Paktika, and Kandahar.[18]

Figure 2.2 shows the primary targets of insurgents. Women have frequently been targeted for a variety of reasons, including running girls' schools. The Taliban have bombed schools and assassinated teachers because they oppose education for girls. One night letter left at a school in Wardak warned, "Respected Afghans: Abandon the culture and traditions of the Christians and Jews. Do not send your girls to school." Otherwise, it noted, the Taliban "will conduct their robust military operations in the daylight."[19] Women have also been targeted

Figure 2.2
Primary Insurgent Targets, 2002–2006

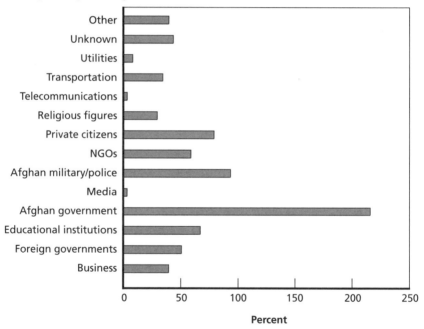

RAND *MG579-2.2*

---

[18] "Country Risk Assessment: Afghanistan," 2004; Bhatia, Lanigan, and Wilkinson, 2004, pp. 1–8; Davis, 2003, pp. 10–15.

[19] Coursen-Neff, 2006. For attacks on schools, also see Human Rights Watch (2006).

during election campaigns, with the Taliban arguing that "the elections are a part of the American program" and those who participate in the elections "are the enemies of Islam and the homeland."[20] Masooda Jalal, the only female presidential candidate during the 2004 election campaign, received numerous death threats.[21] Additionally, insurgents strongly disapprove of Afghan women working for international organizations and NGOs and have threatened and targeted them.

Crime

Women have been targets of criminal violence, defined by the United Nations as "any act of gender-based violence that results in, or is likely to result in, physical, sexual, or psychological harm or suffering to women, including threats of such acts, coercion or arbitrary deprivation of liberty, whether occurring in public or private life."[22] Public-opinion data in Afghanistan suggest that the most likely crime victims are Shi'ites (27 percent), lower-income women (25 percent), Hazaras (21 percent), and women with less than primary school education (16 percent).[23] According to a 2003 report by Amnesty International, women in rural areas, where 85 percent of the population lives, feared roving militia groups. Lawlessness in these regions made "their lives worse than [it was] during the Taliban era."[24]

Data on rape are difficult to acquire in Afghanistan. Women rarely report rape because of the social stigma attached to the victim and her family, ineffective investigation mechanisms, and the failure of the state or local tribes to provide justice to victims. Women fear imprisonment, harassment, and discrimination from the police for reporting rape—as well as rejection or violent reactions from their own families.

---

[20] Afghan Islamic Press interview with Mofti Latifollah Hakimi, August 30, 2005.

[21] Amnesty International, 2004b.

[22] United Nations Development Fund for Women, 1994.

[23] In these data, victims are categorized according to a number of criteria, including ethnic group, gender, and economic status. The first three categories do not include women (Asia Foundation, 2004, p. 25).

[24] Amnesty International, 2003.

Nonetheless, organizations such as Amnesty International have documented many cases of rape and domestic abuse.[25]

Domestic Violence

Violence against women by family members is widespread and includes deprivation of education and economic opportunities, verbal and psychological violence, beatings, sexual violence, and murder. Many acts of violence are the result of traditional practices, including the betrothal of young girls in infancy, early marriage, forced marriage, and crimes of "honor" (in which a female is punished for having purportedly offended custom, tradition, or honor). From infancy, girls and women are under the authority of their father or husband, have restricted freedom of movement, face restrictions on their choice of husbands, and have limited possibilities of asserting their economic and social independence. Most women, both unmarried and married, are faced with the stark reality of enduring abuse. Should they try to extricate themselves from the situation of abuse, they invariably face stigma and isolation, as well as possible imprisonment for leaving the home.[26] The United Nations Development Fund for Women has found that cultural factors associated with higher levels of family and community violence include sexual double standards, rigid gender roles, lack of access to education, women's isolation and lack of support, community attitudes that tolerate physical "punishment" of women and children, and acceptance of violence as an appropriate means of resolving conflict.[27]

Forced marriages are also common in Afghanistan.[28] These are distinct from arranged marriages, in which both individuals consent to a marriage arranged by members of their families, an accepted, traditional practice throughout South Asia. Forced marriage is defined

---

[25] For information on specific cases of rape and domestic abuse, see Amnesty International, 2004b; Amnesty International, 2005b.

[26] Amnesty International, 2005b.

[27] United Nations Development Fund for Women, 2003.

[28] Some argue that forced marriages are illegal under Afghan law. However, there is some dispute about what "Afghan law" is, since it incorporates both formal and informal law. See, for example, Chapters 7 and 8 of the Afghan Criminal Code (1976).

as marriage "conducted without the valid consent of both parties and may involve coercion, mental abuse, emotional blackmail, and intense family or social pressure. In the most extreme cases, it may also involve physical violence, abuse, abduction, detention, and murder of the individual concerned."[29]

The Justice System

Women have been notably impacted by a weak and ineffective justice system.[30] Security-sector reform in Afghanistan was based on a "lead nation" approach. The United States was the lead nation for reconstructing the Afghan National Army; Germany, for the police; the United Kingdom, for counternarcotics efforts; Japan (with United Nations assistance), for the disarmament, demobilization, and reintegration of former combatants; and Italy, for justice. In theory, each lead nation was supposed to contribute significant financial assistance, coordinate external assistance, and oversee reconstruction efforts in its sector. In practice, the lead-nation approach did not work as well as envisioned. This has been particularly true of the justice sector, where Italy faced significant hurdles in trying to coordinate reconstruction efforts by a variety of states, NGOs, and large international organizations such as the United Nations.

Efforts to rebuild the justice system were also obstructed by several other factors. The first factor was the central government's inability to decrease the power of warlords and exert control over the country. Warlord commanders, who were allowed to maintain *de facto* control over areas seized following the overthrow of the Taliban regime, established their personal authority over local courts. This factional control of the courts led to intimidation of centrally appointed judges. The second factor that decreased the effectiveness of the justice system was the Afghan government's inability and unwillingness to address

---

[29] Salish and Gah, 2000.

[30] Seth G. Jones, interview with Deputy Minister of Justice Mohammad Qasim Hashimzai, Kabul, Afghanistan, 2004; Jones interview with Carlos Batori, Counselor and Deputy Head of Mission, Italian Government, Kabul, Afghanistan, 2004; Amnesty International, 2005a; Mani, 2003; Miller and Perito, 2004.

widespread and deep-rooted corruption. Corruption was endemic in the system, partly because unqualified personnel loyal to various factions had been installed as court officials. The Supreme Court and the Attorney General's Office were accused of significant corruption.[31] The World Bank stated that Afghanistan's government was one of the most corrupt in the world.[32]

The corrupt and poorly functioning justice system had a strongly negative effect on the condition of women. At all levels of the criminal-justice system, the authorities failed to respond to women's complaints of domestic violence, rape, sexual violence, or other assaults. Prosecutors generally refused to open investigations into cases involving domestic violence or to order protective measures for women who were at risk from their family or the community. Indeed, the deputy prosecutor in Kandahar informed Amnesty International that his office had never received any reports of violence against women and that such violence no longer occurred since the fall of the Taliban regime.[33] Complaints from victims of domestic violence are widely dismissed by the police as private matters, and victims are often advised (and sometimes pressured) to return to their abusive spouses and families. The high level of discrimination against women is reflected in the fact that violence against women is not necessarily seen as relevant grounds for seeking or granting a divorce. Access to a divorce is an essential remedy against violence, and the absence of it contributes to the continuation of violence against women.

The police are reluctant to prevent and investigate family violence, including the violent deaths of girls. When women have sought assistance after suffering violence or escaping forced marriages, the police have often sent them home, accusing them of tarnishing their families' reputations. Alternatively, the police routinely imprison women, supposedly for their own protection.[34] The right of accused persons

---

[31] Seth G. Jones interview with Deputy Minister of Justice Mohammad Qasim Hashimzai, Kabul, Afghanistan, June 26, 2004; Mani, 2003, p. 2.

[32] Kaufmann, Kraay, and Mastruzzi, 2004.

[33] Amnesty International, 2005b.

[34] Ibid.

to legal assistance of their choosing is crucial for the fairness of any trial. However, access to legal defense is severely compromised for many, if not most, women in Afghanistan. Legal representation for detained and accused women is almost nonexistent. Women seeking legal aid are perceived to be acting outside accepted codes of behavior. Some NGOs have begun to address this issue. The international NGO Medica Mondiale, for example, established a project providing legal aid to some female prisoners in Kabul, since most had not been provided legal representation by the state.[35] As an additional problem, female human-rights advocates face prejudice from a predominantly male judiciary. One judge remarked to a female advocate during the trial of three women accused of *zina* (unlawful sexual activity), "You must be a bad woman yourself for wanting to defend those three bad women."[36]

The Impact of Women on Security

Thus far, we have discussed the negative consequences of the post-conflict situation for women. We will now look at the ways in which women have played an important role in the security environment. In general, this role has not been well understood, which has led to a tendency to overlook its significance.

For insurgent groups, popular support is an overriding strategic objective. As Mao Tse-tung argued, "The richest source of power to wage war lies in the masses of the people."[37] Consequently, to defeat the Taliban and other insurgents in Afghanistan, their support base must be curbed. Governance—including broader reconstruction efforts—is a critical component of this strategy and is highly correlated with the success of counterinsurgency efforts.[38] Governance involves the provision of essential services to the population by a central authority in a

---

[35] Medica Mondiale, 2006.

[36] Medica Mondiale, 2004, p. 13.

[37] Mao Tse-tung, 1963, p. 260.

[38] Fearon and Laitin, 2003.

timely manner.[39] Poor governance may indicate disorganization and weakness, and thus an opportunity for insurgents to win popular support. Women have played an important role in governance and security efforts and have been helpful in winning popular support away from insurgents in the eastern and southern provinces of Afghanistan. Women's role has been significant in three areas: civil affairs; disarmament, demobilization, and reintegration; and security forces.

Civil Affairs

A key women's role in civil affairs has been cooperation with the U.S.- and NATO-led Provincial Reconstruction Teams (PRTs) and Team Village missions. The PRTs generally consist of approximately 60 to 100 soldiers and are made up of civil-affairs units, Special Forces, force-protection units, and psychological-operations personnel. The U.S. PRTs also include a small number (less than a half-dozen) of State Department, United States Agency for International Development (USAID), and other U.S. government personnel. The PRTs facilitate reconstruction by funding projects such as school repairs and by helping the State Department, USAID, and U.S. Department of Agriculture representatives implement civilian projects.[40] Team Village missions comprising a mix of U.S. and coalition civil-affairs and psychological-operations personnel conduct civil-military operations within a larger campaign. Many also include tactical human-intelligence teams, interpreters, military police, media and public-affairs personnel, medical personnel, and local Afghan forces.[41]

Both the PRTs and the Team Village missions view women as key beneficiaries of their programs, especially in areas such as health services. These programs are of particular benefit to Afghan women, because they face the highest rates of illiteracy and the lowest standards of health in the world. Health-care operations are particularly welcome, and day clinics offered by U.S. and coalition forces always

---

[39] On governance, see Kaufmann, Kraay, and Mastruzzi (2004), Kaufmann (2005–2006), Paris (2004).

[40] Borders, 2004; McNerney, 2005–2006.

[41] U.S. Army Training and Doctrine Command, 2004, p. 12; Buffaloe, 2004, pp. 13–14.

have lines of patients.[42] As noted earlier, many women have been so thankful for the health care they received from U.S. military forces for themselves and their children that they have been willing to assist in the fight against insurgents.

The effective use of PRTs and Team Village missions may be one reason why public-opinion polls in Afghanistan showed fairly high levels of support for the United States and the Afghan government in the early phases of the counterinsurgency campaign.[43] Roughly 65 percent of Afghans responding to a poll in 2004 had a favorable view of the U.S. government, and 67 percent had a favorable view of the U.S. military. About 85 percent of those interviewed had a "very favorable" or "somewhat favorable" view of President Hamid Karzai.[44]

However, there are several indications that support for the United States, coalition forces, and the Afghan government began to decline in 2006, as levels of violence rose and frustration with the pace of reconstruction increased. Amrullah Saleh, head of the National Directorate for Security, concluded that the Taliban had won popular support in the east and south and succeeded in setting up a foothold in such provinces as Helmand and Kandahar:

> [A] lot of people in the villages of Zabul, Helmand, Kandahar, and Oruzgan . . . say this is a corrupt government. They also say you are the government and we are the people. This black and white explanation must change.[45]

Disarmament, Demobilization, and Reintegration

Afghan women have been at the forefront of calls to disarm private militias. They have organized protests and signed petitions, even at var-

---

[42] When the counterinsurgency effort began, U.S. forces received information that some villages did not want humanitarian assistance because insurgents threatened to retaliate if villages accepted help from them. In response, the U.S. forces left hidden stay-behind observation posts to monitor and attack those who went into the village after they departed. For more on the high rate of acceptance of medical aid, see Gall (2007).

[43] On Afghanistan and public opinion, see "ABC News Poll: Life in Afghanistan" (2005), Courtney et al. (2005), Asia Foundation (2004), International Republican Institute (2004a).

[44] Asia Foundation, 2004, pp. 107–108.

[45] Saleh, 2006.

ious Loya Jirgas. Women called for disarmament in the Afghan Women's Bill of Rights, as well as in the Declaration of Afghan Women's NGOs.[46] Women have also played a direct role in the disarmament, demobilization, and reintegration of combatants. The United Nations Afghanistan New Beginnings Programme (ANBP) provided direct services to women and children who were combatants. By mid-2006, 24,536 women had received education and income-generation opportunities in development projects. The World Food Programme (WFP) signed a letter of intent to facilitate the inclusion of 4,455 women from the ex-combatant community in WFP-related projects from 2006 to 2010. In addition, 153,915 ex-combatant children received assistance through WFP's Food for Education assistance programs.[47]

Security Forces

There has been limited progress in integrating women directly into the Afghan National Security Forces. Soon after the Taliban government was overthrown, the Afghan government decided to build a police force that included both men and women, so women have been more successful in integrating into the police. As the *National Development Framework 2002* noted:

> The overarching goal is to create a national police force to ensure security throughout Afghanistan and to contribute to regional and global security. . . . The police academy will be revived and *men and women* who are graduates of high school will be chosen on the basis of a competitive exam.[48]

The first team of German police trainers arrived in Kabul in March 2002 to train police instructors. Training was critical, since Afghan police had not received formal training for at least two decades.[49] At the police academy in Kabul, the Germans focused on training inspectors

---

[46] Sultan, 2005, p. 22.

[47] United Nations Development Programme, 2006.

[48] Afghan Interim Administration, 2002, p. 47 (emphasis added).

[49] Benard et al., 2003, p. 6; Asian Development Bank and World Bank, 2002, p. 7.

and lieutenants. Officers went through a three-year course and took classes on human rights, tactical operations, narcotics investigations, traffic, criminal investigations, computer skills, and Islamic law.[50]

By 2003, however, U.S. officials at the State Department, Defense Department, and White House became increasingly unhappy with the German approach. Many argued that it was far too slow, trained too few police officers, and was seriously underfunded.[51] Consequently, the United States stepped in to begin training constable-level male and female recruits at the central training center in Kabul, as well as at regional training centers in such cities as Kandahar, Mazar-e Sharif, Gardez, and Jalalabad. The Bureau of International Narcotics and Law Enforcement Affairs (INL) contracted with DynCorp to train police and to help build training facilities.[52] Beginning in 2005, the U.S. military took over the lead police role.

The presence of women was deemed critical to the police force, since they were necessary for such tasks as guarding female prisoners and searching female suspects. But no comparable rationale was seen for the Army. Although women were trained at U.S. and German police training facilities in Kabul and throughout the country at regional training centers, they still failed to secure top-level appointments in the Ministry of Interior or in the Afghan National Police. This was largely due to opposition in the Afghan presidential palace and the Ministry of Interior to allowing women to play leadership roles in what was viewed as a male profession.

---

[50] Seth G. Jones, interview with Jochen Rieso, Training Branch, German Project for Support of the Police in Afghanistan, Kabul, Afghanistan, June 27, 2004.

[51] According to one high-level U.S. official, "When it became clear that they were not going to provide training to lower-level police officers, and were moving too slowly with too few resources, we decided to intervene to prevent the program from failing" (Seth G. Jones, interview with senior U.S. official, White House, September 2004). This view was corroborated in multiple interviews with U.S. officials in Washington and Afghanistan in 2004 and 2005.

[52] Seth G. Jones, interview with members of DynCorp, Kabul and Gardez, June 2004; interview with members of DynCorp, Kabul, November 2005.

Meanwhile, there have been virtually no women in the Afghan National Army (ANA). The United States was the lead nation for building the ANA, although instructors from France, Turkey, and other coalition countries have also been involved.[53] Training commenced in May 2002, when the ANA's first regular battalion began ten weeks of infantry and combat training at the Kabul Military Training Center. U.S. Special Operations forces assigned to the 1st Battalion, 3rd Special Forces Group, provided the initial training.[54] Combined Security Transition Command–Afghanistan staff, including Task Force Phoenix, then took over the bulk of the ANA training. New Afghan recruits received training on basic rifle marksmanship, platoon- and company-level tactics, use of heavy weapons, and engineering, scout, and medical skills. But women have played little role in the construction or makeup of the ANA. By 2006, fewer than 200 women were serving in the ANA, all in medical, logistics, and communications positions. The ANA did not recruit women for service as entry-level soldiers, and only men served in combat and combat-support units.[55]

The United States and other Western governments made no effort to encourage the inclusion of women in the military. Interviews with Afghan Ministry of Defense officials and U.S. soldiers involved in ANA training indicated that the reason was straightforward: Fighting has traditionally been viewed in Afghanistan as a job for males.[56] During three decades of civil war that began in 1979, men and boys have been the primary combatants. As Maj. Gen. Homayun Fawzi, the assistant Afghanistan Minister of Defense for Personnel and Education, argued, "In principle we concur with women serving in the [Afghan National

---

[53] Seth G. Jones visited the Office of Military Cooperation–Afghanistan in 2004, the Office of Security Cooperation–Afghanistan in 2005, the Combined Security Transition Command–Afghanistan in 2006, and regional training centers during that period to assess the U.S. and coalition efforts to rebuild the ANA and the Afghan National Police. On training of the ANA, also see Manuel and Singer, 2002; F. Hill, 2003, p. 6.

[54] Davis, 2002; Sedra, 2002, pp. 28–30.

[55] Seth G. Jones, interview with Afghan Ministry of National Defense officials, Kabul, Afghanistan, September 2006.

[56] Seth G. Jones, interview with Afghan Ministry of Defense and U.S. Department of Defense officials, Kabul and Kandahar, Afghanistan, January 2007.

Army]. But the service of women must be discussed and planned to determine the career fields and branches in which they may serve based on Afghan culture and norms."[57]

In sum, women have played a notable role in security. They have cooperated with Afghan, U.S., and other NATO military forces through the PRTs and Team Village missions. They have participated in disarmament, demobilization, and reintegration and, to a limited degree, in policing. They have also played an important role in managing interethnic tension. During the Constitutional Loya Jirga, for example, women signed requests by the Uzbek minority to gain official status for their language in regions where it was most widely spoken. They did this in exchange for Uzbek support for increasing women's representation in government.[58]

Despite these successes, however, there is need for caution, because there are some drawbacks to a heightened role for women, particularly in the security sector, where women identified with the new government and the normative changes it represents have been especially targeted. For example, Safiye Amajan, the provincial head of the Ministry of Women's Affairs, was assassinated. Similarly, schools that educate girls have been regularly targeted in the south and east.[59] This is an enduring and perhaps inevitable reality in transitioning societies.

Recommendations

Security and women have a double-edged relationship in Afghanistan. While security lapses in the form of social and economic insecurity, insurgent attacks, crime, and inadequate access to justice remain significant, women are a great potential source of peace and stability for Afghanistan. This suggests that long-term security in Afghanistan will be a function of both decreasing the violence against women and

---

[57] Kai, 2005.

[58] Sultan, 2005, p. 25.

[59] Amnesty International, Afghanistan, 2006; Human Rights Watch, 2006; Coursen-Neff, 2006.

increasing the positive contributions of women in establishing peace. This leads to three major recommendations.

First, Afghan authorities should be encouraged to publicly and unequivocally condemn all violence against women and girls, including violence in the family. Since no comprehensive data exist on violence against women in Afghanistan, an additional step should be to collect data and compile statistics on it. This information must be made publicly available. It should cover such issues as the causes of violence against women, including social attitudes, customs, and practice. Supporting research should examine the effects of such violence, the effectiveness of measures to counter it, and the social attitudes underlying it. This research could be done by an international organization such as the United Nations or by any of several relevant NGOs in Afghanistan.

Second, international actors should continue to support and encourage reform of the criminal-justice system. Under the increased weight of blowback violence, clearly discernible in 2007, the solution must be the effective integration of the rule of law to combat and curb violent activity. This should include comprehensive training of the judiciary and police to implement international law and standards that promote the rights of women. It could also include modifying or abolishing existing laws (such as the penal code), regulations, customs, and practices that constitute discrimination against women in family matters. In particular, reform of the criminal-justice system should ensure that women are given legal equality with men in law and in practice—as the Afghan constitution requires. This will be particularly necessary in ensuring the right to freely choose a spouse, the right to enter into marriage only with full and free consent, and equal rights and responsibilities during marriage and its dissolution. Furthermore, Afghan authorities must ensure that the law is implemented by the courts in a way that ensures equality in practice between men and women. Completion of this task at the outset of reconstruction might have proactively prevented the highly volatile and responsive surge in violence we see in today's efforts by a minority to re-Talibanize the society through intimidation and force.

Third, Afghan women and their nascent humanitarian organizations need to continue playing their critical role in service delivery and to participate in the processes of governance. They have already provided assistance in education, health care, and availability of clean water.[60] These governance and reconstruction efforts are especially critical in the south and east, where the Taliban and other insurgent groups have been most active. They give women an important opportunity to curb the power of insurgents and to build support for the Afghan government. Indeed, the long-term hope for peace in Afghanistan depends to an important degree on the role of women.

---

[60] Sultan, 2005, p. xi.

CHAPTER THREE

Planning and Implementing Programs for Women's Health and Education: Building Indicators of Success

This chapter examines the vital issue of planning and data mechanisms in the nation-building context, highlighting the role of health and education indicators. Such mechanisms provide feedback regarding ongoing nation-building programs and guide policy choices and resource allocations for the future. These determinants, when collected with precision and focus, are crucial to the continual redefining of the scope and goals of the nation-building mission. Moreover, development of best practices for such data collection and assessment could successfully integrate women at all levels of the policy-planning process.

The chapter begins with an overview of useful current data regarding women in Afghanistan; however, the big picture is far from complete. In fact, that picture is rarely available in conflict and post-conflict zones, due to the stark inconsistencies and unavailability of data—the subject of this chapter's latter portion.

The Current Outlook for Women in Afghanistan

Many local and international organizations are working to improve the lives of women and children in post-conflict Afghanistan. While the "heavy hitters" in the international community, particularly the United States, tend to focus on security, political participation, and economic opportunities for adults in post-conflict nation-building,

many smaller international and local organizations are looking specifically to improve the lives of women and children. However, some basic
data collected by the United Nations Children's Fund (UNICEF) for
Afghanistan, shown in Table 3.1, illustrate the seemingly insurmount-
able task facing these organizations: The UNICEF data paint a stark
picture for women and girls in Afghanistan in the past five years. Only
half as many girls as boys are enrolled in primary school. This disparity continues into secondary school, where gross enrollment rates show
that even fewer girls make it to that level, although the numbers of
boys also decrease severely. The gross enrollment rates shown are based
on the number of children enrolled in a level (primary or secondary),
regardless of age, divided by the population of the age group that officially corresponds to the same level. In 2005, UNICEF launched a

Table 3.1
Statistics on Women in Afghanistan

Item	Percent
Enrollment ratios: females as a percentage of males, primary school (2000–2005[a]), net	53
Secondary-school enrollment ratio 2000–2005,[a] gross, male	25
Secondary-school enrollment ratio 2000–2005,[a] gross, female	5
Adult literacy rate, 2000–2004,[a] male	43
Adult literacy rate, 2000–2004,[a] female	13
Contraceptive prevalence, 1996–2004[a]	10
Antenatal-care coverage, 1996–2004[a]	16
Skilled attendant at delivery, 1996–2004[a]	14
Reported maternal mortality ratio,[b] 1990–2004[a]	1,600
Adjusted maternal mortality ratio,[b] 2000	1,900
Maternal mortality ratio (lifetime risk of maternal death), 2000	16

SOURCE: United Nations Children's Fund, "Information by Country," online at http://
www.unicef.org/infobycountry/afghanistan_afghanistan_statistics.html (as of October 25, 2007).

[a]Data refer to the most recent year available during the period specified in the column
heading on the web site.

[b]The maternal mortality data are reported by national authorities. Periodically, UNICEF,
the World Health Organization (WHO), and the United Nations Fund for Population
Activities (UNFPA) evaluate these data and make adjustments to account for the well-
documented problems of underreporting and misclassification of maternal deaths
and to develop estimates for countries with no data. The adjusted estimates for the
year 2000 reflect the most recent of these reviews.

program with the Ministry of Education to increase the number of girls in school.[1] According to data reported by Afghanistan Online, a clear majority—60 percent—of school-age girls were not attending classes. The figure in Southern Afghanistan was 90 percent. School attendance for boys and girls in Afghanistan severely lags behind that in neighboring countries such as Pakistan, Iran, and Uzbekistan and is more comparable to countries located in sub-Saharan Africa, such as Benin, Chad, and Burundi.[2] The lack of schooling for Afghan children contributes directly to Afghanistan's stark illiteracy rates, also shown in Table 3.1. The World Bank's GenderStats database reports that the adult female literacy rate for Afghanistan is 12 percent for women 15 years of age and older and only 18 percent for women 15 to 24 years of age, a cohort that under better circumstances might have shown stronger benefits from the past six years.

Prenatal care is also very poor in Afghanistan, where only 16 percent of women are seen by a skilled professional even once during pregnancy, and a record 1,600 women per 100,000 die during childbirth. The World Bank reports a very high birth rate, 7.2 births per woman in Afghanistan, and a fertility rate among girls aged 15 to 19 of 117 percent. The World Bank also reports that 40 percent of Afghan children under five years of age are malnourished.[3] Again, the rates in Afghanistan are closer to those in African nations such as Chad than to those in neighboring countries.[4]

---

[1] United Nations Office of Coordination of Humanitarian Affairs, "New Campaign to Encourage Girls into School," online at http://www.afghan-web.com/woman/encouragegirlsschool.html (as of October 25, 2007).

[2] UNICEF, "State of the World's Children 2007," Table 5: Education, online at http://www.unicef.org/sowc07/docs/sowc07_table_5.pdf (as of October 25, 2007).

[3] Additional data available on women in Afghanistan at the World Bank's GenderStats web site, http://genderstats.worldbank.org/genderRpt.asp?rpt=profile&cty=AFG,Afghanistan&hm=home3 (as of October 25, 2007).

[4] UNICEF, "State of the World's Children 2007," Table 3: Health, online at http://www.unicef.org/sowc07/docs/sowc07_table_3.pdf (as of October 25, 2007).

Making the Case for Improved Data Collection on Women in Postwar Reconstruction

Except for the data provided by UNICEF and the World Bank, there are no systematically collected databases on women and children in Afghanistan, as is also the case for many conflict-torn countries in the world. Without baseline data from which to measure improvements, it is impossible to know whether nation-building efforts to improve the lives of women and children are successful. In Afghanistan, as in many similar conflicts, because of the overwhelming scope of the problem, NGOs such as Afghanistan Online, Women for Afghan Women (WAW), and other indigenous advocacy organizations put their limited resources into programming and outreach activities instead of data collection. The limited data collected by such organizations are not organized or analyzed in a central location and therefore may not be comparable. Often, data are collected only on women who receive services from a program, and no attempt is made to provide a larger picture of women's health or education in general. In other words, the data that may be available may not be comparable, appropriately collected through any acknowledged sampling methodology, made known to the national government, or deposited with the intervening organization or the international community. This leads to the common problem of the "right hand not knowing what the left is doing." Without a centralized data-collection authority, data that are collected are either lost or collected in ways that make them less actionable. Data collection in individual conflict zones by groups other than the major international organizations such as UNICEF and the United Nations Educational, Scientific and Cultural Organization (UNESCO) is unlikely to be done correctly, if at all.

The problems of data collection in Afghanistan illustrate the difficulty of culling available data for indicators pertaining to women in nation-building. We are seeking globally based, comparative data that will enable us to compare policies in different post-conflict situations, so the best data sources would ordinarily be international agencies such as the United Nations Statistics Division and the World Bank. However, even these well-known statistical repositories often fail to contain usable data for conflict zones because the established reporting regimes are either corrupted or disrupted. For example, in the decade leading up to the post-9/11 U.S. invasion of Afghanistan, data on a variety of health and education indicators were not collected or reported. It was not until after 9/11 that objective observers from the United Nations Development Programme (UNDP) were able to begin collecting data on Afghan women's lives.[5]

The lack of reliable data on Afghanistan has slowed reconstruction work because solid plans cannot be crafted until the international community has intervened and created a baseline understanding on which to form policies. Further, the accuracy of these policies cannot be pragmatically determined, because change cannot be measured. It is clear that the sooner reliable data can be collected for a population in conflict, the faster policy plans can be crafted, implemented, and evaluated. Since international organizations such as UNDP, UNESCO, and UNICEF set the standard for data collection, their activities should be integrated into post-conflict stability and reconstruction operations so that data collection can continue, baselines can be created, policy guidance can be issued, and programs can be measured. It would also be worthwhile for international agencies to consider ways in which data collection, at least on some fundamental matters, can be ongoing even during times of crisis. For example, it was traditional in Afghanistan to observe ceasefires during annual vaccination campaigns. Similar windows of opportunity can perhaps be found for data collection during exceptional times. This would require creativity in assessment and reporting mechanisms, but the time saved and the increase of efficacy gained by jump-starting post-conflict programs would make such an effort worthwhile.

Many organizations are beginning to realize the importance of reliable data collection. Security Council Resolution 1325 calls for collecting data on women and children in war, and the U.S. State Department's Office of the Coordinator for Reconstruction and Stabilization (S/CRS) identifies data collection as one of many "essential tasks" in

---

[5] United Nations Development Programme, 2004a; United Nations, Statistics Division, 2006.

the "social well-being" category. The Essential Task Matrix[6] identifies data collection as a necessary basis for assessment, analysis, and reporting, to support a baseline in order to evaluate any intervention. The matrix highlights five data collection tasks:

1. Identify what critical information is needed, where to find it, what major gaps exist, and how to share, present, and disseminate the information. If possible, conduct this assessment in advance and identify the gaps in data, information, and knowledge.
2. Collect information that can provide situational awareness (e.g., conditions on the ground; severity indicators; affected populations; location and numbers of affected populations; damage assessments; security assessments).
3. Collect information that can provide operational or programmatic information (e.g., logistical access routes; "who's doing what where"; program/financial needs of organizations; who are other donors).
4. Collect information for background knowledge (e.g., history; geography; population demographics and composition; baseline health indicators; political and economic structure and status; infrastructure; culture of the country).
5. Analyze information in context; relate it to other thematic information; evaluate issues and responses; make projections about the future; recommend policies and actions.

This "essential task" list is located in the matrix under social well-being, but these tasks should be applied to all other areas of the matrix. How can a post-conflict reconstruction project be judged if not through a rigorous review of data in the targeted population? If a baseline is not created and measured against specific goals and targets, assessment of progress will be measured by the news media, whose selection and reporting standards often differ significantly from those of social scientists, or by women's advocacy groups, which have a much narrower focus.

---

[6] U.S. Department of State, 2005a.

Table 3.2 shows the main "essential tasks" listed by S/CRS that measure social well-being and other areas that might support women's participation in post-conflict reconstruction.

As explained in Chapter One, these categories are not only the most important to women's well-being, they are also the most important for the well-being of the entire society. Thus, measuring change in these tasks is a way to gauge the reconstruction progress of the society as a whole.

Recent Improvements in Measuring Gains for Women and Girls in Education and Health

Health and education are mutually supporting indicators of women's well-being in society. Without health, women and girls cannot participate in school or work to support their families. And without school, women and girls do not have the requisite knowledge and skills to participate effectively in society or to contribute to the well-being of their families and communities. Thus, it is somewhat artificial to treat health and education separately. This insight is supported by several recent developments in data collection, which favor creating indexes that target women's health and education jointly. Single indicators of

Table 3.2
Areas That May Support Women's Participation in Post-Conflict Reconstruction Tasks

Governance and participation • Elections and political parties	Economic stabilization and infrastructure • Employment generation • Agriculture development
Humanitarian assistance and social well-being • Refugees and internally displaced personss • Trafficking in persons • Food security • Shelter and non-food relief • Humanitarian de-mining • Public health • Education • Social protection • Assessment, analysis, and reporting	• Social safety net • Telecommunications • Energy Justice and reconciliation • Legal-system reform • Human rights • Truth commissions and remembrance • Community rebuilding

health or education, such as access to basic services, do not tell the whole story. Rather, researchers in gender and development have moved steadily from conceptualizing women's progress from basic output indicators, such as how many girls attend school, to the human-development approach, which focuses on creating measures for women in the context of their overall standing in society.[7]

This does not mean that single statistics are not useful—in fact, school data have been disaggregated according to gender, an action that provided very important information for development planners, only since the 1990s. However, there are simply no internationally rec-ognized indicators that focus on more-qualitative outcomes for gender in health and education. For example, data on the quality of infrastruc-ture and facilities, numbers of textbooks and supplies, teaching materi-als, and exam results are not collected universally for children, let alone disaggregated for girls and boys.

Education Statistics

Schools are critical to post-conflict reconstruction. They not only bring a sense of normalcy to children in war-torn areas, they also offer adults a chance to see a functioning system that is working toward rebuilding a sense of community and hope for the future of their children. Open and functioning schools offer children a respite from damaged homes and conflict-induced poverty. They offer teachers the opportunity to become agents of change in their communities, and they give them employment and salaries.[8] To the extent that schools remove children and youths from the streets, they may help reduce the likelihood of their being drawn into criminal or insurgent activities, especially if the schools also succeed in transmitting positive civic values, practical life skills, and a real hope of a future vocation and livelihood. For all of these reasons, it is appropriate that in the U.S. State Department's

---

[7] For a description of the historical development of frameworks, see Unterhalter, Challender, and Rajagopalan (2005).

[8] Kirk, 2005.

essential tasks for education in post-conflict reconstruction, shown in Table 3.3, the opening of schools is shown as a critical and immediate task. The S/CRS essential tasks for education divide initial and long-term tasks into three main categories: personnel, facilities, and curriculum. The curriculum targets diversity training, and an additional

Table 3.3
Essential Tasks for Education in Post-Conflict Reconstruction

Task	Initial Response: Provide Emergency Humanitarian Needs	Transformation: Establish Foundation for Development	Fostering Sustainability: Institutionalize Long-Term Development Program
Human resources	Reopen schools as quickly as possible; use them to reach civil populace with programs	Identify and recruit teachers and administrators; register school-aged population; create equal-opportunity education policy	Train teachers and administrators
Education–schools	Evaluate needs for new schools; build and repair schools; obtain educational materials	Open schools	Maintain and enlarge new or restored schools
Education–universities	Evaluate needs for new universities; build and repair universities; obtain educational materials	Open universities	Maintain and enlarge new or restored universities
Curriculum		Develop curriculum that respects diversity	Distribute curriculum and supporting teaching materials
Literacy campaign	Survey literacy levels and linguistic groups; develop literacy campaign	Conduct literacy campaign	Institutionalize opportunities for adult education to sustain efforts for literacy campaign

SOURCE: U.S. Department of State, Office of the Coordinator for Reconstruction and Stabilization, 2005b.

literacy campaign task is attached to the list. The matrix focuses on registering students, hiring teachers, building and repairing buildings, obtaining materials, and developing literacy and diversity curricula. Plans for sustaining these activities rely on more of the same.

The task matrix seems a half-hearted attempt to throw pen to paper rather than a legitimate plan of action for rebuilding an entire school system for a war-torn nation. The tasks as outlined are inappropriate and ineffective, especially in view of the enormous progress made in understanding and fostering new approaches to increasing educational opportunities for women and girls.

A greater problem beyond opening schools in a post-conflict context is guaranteeing access to education for girls. Globally, two-thirds of those who lack access to education are girls and women. Nearly three-quarters of a billion girls lack access to education.[9] UNESCO's Education for All program states that higher enrollment of girls improves the overall development of a country in the long term. UNESCO research shows that educated women are more likely to lead healthier lives and are better able to advocate for themselves and their children and to contribute to the economic and political fabric of society.[10]

Other organizations also provide basic statistics supporting education for women and girls. The Millennium Development Goals, developed through the United Nations, recognize the powerful impact that education can have on reducing worldwide poverty and instability and could easily be used as general goals for post-conflict reconstruction. Millennium Development Goals 2 and 3 directly address education and girls' access to education as a means of ending poverty. Goal 2 seeks to achieve universal primary education worldwide by ensuring that all boys and girls complete a full course of primary schooling. Goal 3 promotes gender equality and the empowerment of women and calls for eliminating gender disparity in primary and secondary education by 2005, and at all levels by 2015.[11] These goals are internationally

---

[9] Aikman and Unterhalter, 2005.

[10] United Nations Education, Scientific and Cultural Organization, 2005.

[11] United Nations, Millennium Development Goals. As of October 25, 2007: http://www.un.org/millenniumgoals/goals.html.

accepted, having been endorsed by the member states of the United Nations, and therefore should also be used in developing expected outcomes, targets, and goals for education in post-conflict reconstruction scenarios. Applying these preexisting goals would be a far more efficient process than cobbling together a national plan in the wake of a conflict.

Developing a Measurement Plan for Health and Education in Post-Conflict Reconstruction: The Millenium Development Goals

Assessing the social well-being of a nation is a complicated process that involves collecting data on the population in general before specific health and education indicators can be collected. However, we believe the Millennium Development Goals offer a framework that is focused and manageable. In addition, these goals are based on existing data-collection regimes and are therefore a good place to start in crafting a post-conflict data-collection plan for a social-well-being baseline. These goals are beneficial also because many of them are related to the health and social well-being of both women and men.[12]

Table 3.4 shows one way the Millennium Development Goals could be adapted to women's education in post-conflict situations.

Beyond the two basic education indicators selected for Millennium Development Goals 2 and 3 shown in Table 3.4, several organizations have been developing more-sophisticated indexes that measure gender equality in education, including UNESCO's gender-related Education for All (EFA) index, the Global Education Initiative (GEI), Global Monitoring Report (GMR) index, and Education for All Development Index (EDI).

The GEI index was developed by UNESCO for use in the GMRs. It indicates the extent to which boys and girls are equally present at differemt levels of the education system.[13] The GMRs

---

[12] United Nations, Statistics Division, Millennium Development Goal Indicators Database, updated January 18, 2006.

[13] Unterhalter, Challender, and Rajagopalan, 2005.

Table 3.4
Millennium Development Goals 2 and 3 Adapted for Women's and Girls'
Education Indicators

Millennium Goal 2: Achieve universal primary education
Post-conflict target: Ensure that within ten years of conflict intervention, boys and girls will be able to complete a full five years of primary schooling
Indicators:
• Net enrolment ratio of boys and girls in primary education (UNESCO)
• Proportion of boys and girls starting grade 1 who reach grade 5 (UNESCO)
• Literacy rate of women and men 15–24 years of age (UNESCO)

Millennium Goal 3: Promote gender equality and empower women
a. through education
Post-conflict target: Eliminate gender disparity in primary and secondary education and in all levels of education no later than ten years after conflict intervention
Indicators:
• Ratios of girls to boys in primary, secondary, and tertiary education (UNESCO)
• Ratio of literate women to men 15–24 years of age(UNESCO)

---

attempt to measure quality in schools but do not disaggregate data by gender. Four proxy measures for school quality have been developed in the GMRs: pupil/teacher ratios, teachers' qualifications, expenditure on education, and learning achievements for boys and girls.[14] As a starting point for countries undergoing post-conflict reconstruction, the GMR indicators may be sufficient. They measure access to education and the capacity of a school to teach children. However, they do not move toward measuring outcomes of schooling, such as the rate at which children graduate from grade 5. Furthermore, they do not measure outcomes of gender equality, such as rates of boys and girls progressing through school, graduating, and getting jobs in society.

UNESCO's EDI, developed in 2003, attempted to correct for the limitations of the GMR indicators by bringing together data on access, quality, and gender. The EDI consists of the following indicators:

1.   Universal primary education: net enrollment ratio
2.   Adult literacy: literacy rate of persons 15 years of age and over
3.   Gender: gender-specific EFA index as GEI
4.   Progression: survival rate to grade 5

---

[14] Ibid., p. 63.

While the EDI measures the most important input (net enrollment), output (progression through school), and outcome (adult literacy) indicators for educational development and also includes a measure for gender, gender advocates do not believe it goes far enough to include outcomes for women and girls because it does not disaggregate progression through school (output measure) or adult literacy (outcome measure) for girls and women, and the gender component uses the GEI, which measures only enrollment (input measure) in different levels of school.[15]

Unterhalter, Challender, and Rajagopalan (2005), working with Oxfam (a group of NGOs from three continents working worldwide to fight poverty and injustice), propose building a new index that focuses on the concept of capabilities in relation to education outcomes, rather than on outputs of the education system itself. This would bring education indexes more in line with UNDP's Human Development Index (HDI) and the Gender Development Index (GDI).[16] The GDI is a composite index that measures average achievement in the three basic dimensions captured in the HDI—a long and healthy life, knowledge, and a decent standard of living—adjusted to account for inequalities between men and women.[17] The GDI includes the same basic data as the HDI but focuses on the differences between women and men in life expectancy, literacy, and primary, secondary, and tertiary enrollment, as well as in earned income. The GDI is presently available for only 143 countries and does not include most of the countries in the Middle East.[18]

---

[15] Ibid.

[16] For a technical description of Human Development Report indexes and how they are calculated, see Technical Note 1, available at http://hdr.undp.org/reports/global/2000/en/pdf/hdr_2000_back3.pdf (as of October 25, 2007).

[17] United Nations Development Programme, Human Development Reports, available at http://hdr.undp.org/reports/global/2003/indicator/indic_197_1_1.html (as of October 25, 2007).

[18] United Nations Gender Statistics Programme in the Arab Countries, key terms, available at http://www.escwa.org.lb/gsp/main/terms.html (as of October 25, 2007).

Leveraging the spirit of the GDI and the HDI, Unterhalter, Challender, and Rajagopalan propose linking educational achievement with other aspects of gender equality such as health, wealth, and decisionmaking. By limiting the index to a handful of universally (for the most part) collected data, Unterhalter, Challender, and Rajagopalan attempt to create a more outcome-oriented index that is comparable across regions—something that does not currently exist.[19] To achieve this goal, they propose a Gender Equality in Education Index (GEEI), which would gather together data from UNICEF on girls' attendance at school, from UNESCO on girls' achievement in primary school and access to secondary school, and from UNDP's GDI.[20] In this way, the GEEI would assess both access and retention in broader terms by using well-established indicators compiled by leading organizations.

Education indexes such as the EDI or GEEI should be used in conjunction with other indicators for women and girls. In the area of economic and political opportunity, the UNDP's Gender Empowerment Measure (GEM) measures the political and economic empowerment of women relative to that of men by looking at the number/percentage of women in parliament and senior and management positions, as well as the number/percentage of women with professional and technical jobs. The GEM also examines the earned income of women in relation to that of men. However, it is available for only 143 countries, and Egypt is the only Arab country assigned a GEM.[21]

Looking ahead, education indexes should also be paired with indicators for security for women and girls, such as laws criminalizing violence against women[22] and ensuring access to the judicial system.

---

[19] See Chapter Four for a discussion of difficulties of data collection in the Middle East and in countries in conflict.

[20] Unterhalter, Challender, and Rajagopalan, 2005, p. 67.

[21] United Nations Gender Statistics Programme in the Arab Countries, key terms, available at http://www.escwa.org.lb/gsp/main/terms.html (as of October 25, 2007).

[22] International Criminal Court Fact Sheet 7: Ensuring Justice for Women, Amnesty International, available at http://www.amnestyusa.org/icc/document.do?id=962E12D23AAB02 5080256FC700373120 (as of October 25, 2007); also see the Rome Statute of the International Criminal Court, The Hague, http://www.un.org/law/icc/index.html (as of October 25, 2007).

For specific links between education and security, indicators should be developed to measure the danger of sexual harassment and violence at school, girls' anxiety about their future, and discrimination against female teachers.[23]

Millennium Development Goal 3, on empowering women, is a good starting point for developing links between education and political and economic participation by women. Table 3.5 shows two parts of the existing goal and adapts them for women in post-conflict situations.

The Millennium Development Goals help to focus the S/CRS essential-task matrix by prioritizing resources to collect data on selected indicators with specific targets attached to internationally recognized goals. In addition, these goals help to connect other essential elements of society, such as education, economics, politics, and security.

Table 3.5
Millennium Development Goal 3 Adapted for Women in Post-Conflict Situations

A. Through education
Post-conflict target: Eliminate gender disparity in primary and secondary education and in all levels of education no later than ten years after conflict intervention
Indicators:
• Ratios of girls to boys in primary, secondary, and tertiary education (UNESCO)
• Ratio of literate women to men 15–24 years of age (UNESCO)

B. In the workplace
Post-conflict target: Increase the ability of women to compete in jobs outside of the agriculture sector by 50 percent within ten years of conflict intervention
Indicators:
• Share of women in wage employment in the non-agricultural sector (ILO)

C. In the legislature
Post-conflict target: Ensure that 30 percent of the seats in parliament are held by women within five years of conflict intervention
Indicators:
• Proportion of seats held by women in the national parliament (IPU)

NOTE: ILO = International Labor Organization; IPU = Inter-Parliamentary Union.

---

[23] Unterhalter, Challender, and Rajagopalan, 2005, p. 63.

Health Statistics

Post-conflict stability operations also need to take greater interest in women's health. Several reasons argue for this. First, in post-conflict situations, the balance between the male and female populations is often skewed by the deaths of male combatants. Also, as seen in Chapter Two, conflict affects women differently than it affects men. Women are often on the receiving end of violence during conflict and are especially vulnerable to anarchy and elevated levels of domestic violence when combatants return home from the fight.[24] Women's health also tends to be more fragile than men's and more vulnerable to disruptions in health care. Women's health has a direct and causal relationship to the health and survival rates of infants and children. Where women are responsible for the management of the household and for food preparation, their health and also their awareness of hygiene, nutrition, and basic health and first aid practices directly impact not only their own well-being, but also that of the children and men in their families.

As is the case with education statistics, it makes sense to help existing international organizations gain access to post-conflict societies in order to create a baseline of measurement from which to objectively measure progress by the intervening force.

A wide variety of statistics are used to measure the health of an entire society. For example, mortality rates are a key indicator of the effectiveness of health services of a country, just as measures of HIV infection, tuberculosis, and malaria are important in capturing the infectious-disease rates of a population. Still other indicators of health include a population's access to drinking water in urban and rural areas, access to improved sanitation, poverty rates, and public expenditures on health care.

Many indicators for women's health have been collected by a variety of international organizations for a long time. However, the importance of women's health in and of itself is a relatively new focus for the world's health system. For example, it wasn't until 2002 that WHO developed goals focused on women's health (WHO's Gender Policy), largely in response to gender mainstreaming and the Millen-

---

[24] Rehn and Sirleaf, 2002.

nium Development Goals. Because this focus on gender is new, there is no standard set of indicators specifically designed to measure the health of women and girls. Therefore, even though data are collected on many aspects of women's lives, there is no definitive set of indicators to measure progress in women's health. Although there are some very good sources of data, such as the United Nations Statistics Division's database in support of the Millennium Development Goals,[25] the data are generally not well organized. Researchers must wade through the information and double- and triple-check data used by other researchers and organizations before drawing any conclusions. Add to this the difficulty of collecting data on women and girls in conflict zones, and the obstacles facing researchers who would like to set a baseline are immediately apparent.

The international community has made progress in developing indicators for women's health, but many critical international health statistics—for example, statistics on HIV/AIDS, tuberculosis, and malaria—are not disaggregated by gender, even though major international efforts exist to combat these diseases and even though it is known that women and men are impacted differently by them. This makes it very hard to design an effective program.

Finally, some critical health indicators for women simply do not exist. One such indicator is a gender-based violence measure. In February 2006, the United Nations Development Fund for Women (UNIFEM) launched a new database for monitoring violence against women,[26] and WHO suggests indicators of domestic violence such as the rate of homicide by intimate partners (by gender).[27] There is also no universal measure of the rate of unsafe abortions or abortion-related morbidity, an obvious measure of a woman in crisis.[28]

---

[25] This database of information can be searched by country at United Nations, Statistics Division, "Millennium Development Goals," http://millenniumindicators.un.org/unsd/mi/mi.asp (as of October 25, 2007).

[26] United Nations Development Fund for Women in Afghanistan, Violence Against Women, database: http://afghanistan.unifem.org/VAW (as of October 25, 2007).

[27] United Nations Development Fund for Women, 2003.

[28] World Health Organization, 2004.

As is the case with women's education, we believe that the Millennium Development Goals are a good place to start for focusing data collection on women's health in post-conflict reconstruction situations. Table 3.6 shows an adaptation of Millennium Development Goals 4 and 5 for this purpose.

The targets and indicators in Table 3.6 would constitute a more manageable data-collection and measurement endeavor than is currently suggested by the S/CRS Essential Tasks for Health, listed below:

- Potable-water management
- Sanitation and wastewater management
- Medical capacity
- Local public-health clinics
- Hospital facilities
- Human resources development for health-care workforce
- Health policy and financing
- Prevention of epidemics
- HIV/AIDS
- Nutrition
- Reproductive health

Table 3.6
Millennium Development Goals 4 and 5 Adapted for Analysis of Data on Women's Health in Post-Conflict Reconstruction Situations

Millennium Goal 4: Reduce child mortality

Post-conflict target: Reduce the mortality rate of children under five years of age by two-thirds within ten years of conflict intervention

Indicators:
- Under-five mortality rate (UNICEF-WHO)
- Infant mortality rate (UNICEF-WHO)
- Proportion of one-year-old children immunized against measles (UNICEF-WHO)

Millennium Goal 5: Improve maternal health

Post-conflict target: Reduce the maternal mortality rate by three-quarters within ten years of conflict intervention

Indicators:
- Maternal mortality rate (UNICEF-WHO)
- Proportion of births attended by skilled health personnel (UNICEF-WHO)

- Environmental health
- Community health education

The S/CRS Essential Tasks for Health are not well defined or prioritized. Each of the tasks requires a large investment of money and will take time to have an impact. We believe that post-reconstruction authorities should focus health resources on stabilizing maternal and infant health, with all of the tasks associated with that goal, such as ensuring access to potable water and improving sanitation. By stabilizing maternal and infant health, the most basic sector of society would be secured first, allowing women to maintain their families and provide an anchor for reconstructing other elements of their communities. Once the health of a community is stabilized, other health-related activities, such as building medical capacity and facilities and developing long-term programs to improve overall access to health information, can be undertaken.

Collecting Data on Health and Education Indicators for Women and Children in Conflict

In sum, although data on the social well-being of women and children in the world are collected by several leading international organizations, these data are difficult to collect in conflict zones, making it difficult to establish baseline assessments for policy development, and in post-conflict situations, making it difficult to measure progress in reconstruction efforts. In Afghanistan, leading organizations were unable to collect data on health and education during the rule of the Taliban. But even since 2001, it has still been nearly impossible to collect data on more-sophisticated indexes developed by UNESCO, UNDP, Oxfam, and UNICEF. No data are available for UNESCO's EDI for Afghanistan.[29] UNDP has not calculated the GDI for Afghanistan.[30]

---

[29] United Nations Education, Scientific and Cultural Organization, 2005.

[30] United Nations Development Programme, 1994.

And Oxfam's proposed GEEI has not been calculated for Afghanistan or anywhere in the Middle East.

The disconnect between intervening forces and international data-collection organizations should be relatively easy to correct. Intervention forces need the data to gauge their effectiveness, and international organizations need the protection of intervention forces to collect the data. Collaboration between these elements therefore should be a "win-win" situation.

We recommend that any interagency collaboration on women and children's health and education embrace the talents of the United Nations and other international organizations that are already tracking the progress of the world's women and children. There is no need to develop separate goals and targets for a society just because it is in reconstruction after war. On the contrary, it makes more sense to immediately link officials in a war-torn country to as many international systems and organizations as possible to help reconnect the country to the international community.

In countries undergoing post-conflict reconstruction, therefore, data could be collected on indicators in three phases. First, reconstruction efforts should focus on opening the schools and clinics and measuring basic access for girls and boys, women and men. The U.S. military often realizes the importance of such data only years into a conflict and no longer has the ability to obtain a baseline. By starting early and doing the necessary preparation to collect quality data, this mistake can be avoided in the future.[31] The second phase, closely following the first, should focus on bringing in international data-collection organizations such as UNESCO, UNDP, and the World Bank, among others, so that universal data collection on social well-being, using the Millennium Development Goals as a baseline, can begin. A focus on one or two indicators for each area would make it easier to allocate limited resources and help the national government reorganize. Resources must be provided for helping ministries organize and train for data collection. Finally, the reconstruction team must work with the national government, international organizations, and NGOs to develop a data-

---

[31] Unterhalter, Challender, and Rajagopalan, 2005.

collection approach for measuring outcomes in health and education. This could include more-advanced data-collection techniques, such as the national Education Management Information System (EMIS), which is used by most national education ministries and which passes education data on to UNESCO for the compilation of international datasets.

Such a phased approach to health and education, based on objective measures and international data-collection regimes, would have two major benefits. First, it would focus intervention-force and inter-agency resources on establishing access for key sectors of society, such as women and girls, rather than relying on a scattershot approach to rebuilding an entire health or education system. Second, objective measures collected independent of the intervening force would allow a common baseline to be set from which to measure reconstruction progress. This is important for maintaining transparency and accountability within the intervening force, and consequently for enhancing credibility with the international community. More broadly, this phased approach could immediately incorporate the international community into the reconstruction effort, while at the same time linking the country in a meaningful way to other nations.

CHAPTER FOUR

Governance and Women

Conflict challenges the civil-societal infrastructure of a nation, placing further constraints on already marginalized groups and closing avenues for possible protection of rights. In the post-conflict context, nation-builders have an opportunity to establish a credible civil social system (most vitally, state mechanisms of governance and justice) that will reestablish this infrastructure while institutionalizing and mainstreaming women's roles.

Governance encompasses the process of decisionmaking about the management of the state and the delivery of its functions, as well as the way in which those decisions are implemented.[1] In post-conflict settings, the return to peace and normalcy is reflected not only in the gradual resumption of normal state-to-state relations, but also in the manner and extent to which domestic governance is restored and public services providing security, education, health care, and infrastructure—which will often have collapsed or will have been severely degraded during the conflict—are resumed.[2]

A transitional government creates temporary mechanisms to fulfill the most urgent needs until a permanent government can be assembled. During this time period, there is more reliance on external resources, and even the *de facto* management, administration, and decisionmaking may be handled by outsiders. Generally, nation-building includes an effort to build stability by encouraging nascent

---

[1] Anderlini, Conaway, and Keys, 2004.

[2] Dobbins et al., 2007.

governments, even interim governments, to demonstrate their author-ity. This may at times be more of a fiction than a fact, and behind the scenes, governance may be in the hands of international organizations, foreign experts, and the agencies of external governments.

Although there is no lack of literature on best practices for build-ing governance structures in post-conflict settings, the most effective role of women in that process remains vaguely defined and at times contentious.[3] In general, many aspects are entangled in the gender policy followed in nation-building. Women's equality is a cornerstone of the contemporary democratic state, and it is generally thought to be a requisite of any post-conflict government established under the aus-pices of the international community. Women's participation is often also an economic necessity, so that granting women education and training, followed by opportunities commensurate with their talents and skill sets, is the only sensible approach in terms of human capital. Additionally, as beneficiaries of the introduction of more enlightened governance, women can be counted on as voters and as civil-society actors to lend their support to the emerging new government.

On the other side of the equation, though, are forces and influ-ences that agitate against any elevation of women's status. These range from the sincerely held belief that tradition and religion demand the subordination of women or that certain customs objectively detrimen-tal to women are essential for the maintenance of a unique national culture and moral rectitude to a more prosaic desire by men to hold on to perceived advantages and the intertwining of the women's issue with an ideology or value system associated with the enemy. Other disad-vantaged social groups, such as ethnic minorities, often face a similar situation, which will similarly inform efforts to better integrate them and elevate their status.

The process of thinking creatively about the integrated involve-ment of previously marginalized or minority groups must start from the beginning of reconstruction. Some experts recommend that needs-

---

[3] For an excellent and all-encompassing discussion of nation-building best practices see Dobbins et al. (2007).

assessment protocols in governance scenarios work to include women's input.[4]

In 2006, a data-intensive review of state failure and fragility, carried out by the Country Indicators for Foreign Policy Project at Carleton University, found that when ranked by governance indicators, Afghanistan was the world's most fragile state, scoring an index of 9.56 out of 10.[5] Thus, post-conflict Afghanistan provides excellent opportunities to more closely examine the challenges of establishing governance and to examine the potential impacts of the failure to do so.

Historical Context: Patterns of Reform in Afghanistan

Historically, women's rights in Afghanistan have come as a result of what might be called "top down" and "outside in" reform. Both the ideas and the energy driving the change came from elites, who acquired certain new values by being exposed to the ideas of social reformers in the Arab world and in Europe, or through their studies or personal observations abroad. In their efforts to effect change, these individuals were often supported by outside, foreign partners. At other times, the outsiders were themselves the principal agents of the attempted change.

A number of significant reforms were instituted during the rule of progressive King Amanallah and his wife Queen Soraya at the start of the 20th century.[6] Improvements in social services and education for women were important parts of the political platform of Prime Minis-

---

[4] Coleman, 2004c.

[5] Carment et al., 2006. For more on the data, see Country Indicators for Foreign Policy, available at http://www.carleton.ca/cifp/about.htm (as of October 25, 2007).

[6] For example, the queen said in a speech in 1926, "Do not think that our nation needs only men to serve it. Women should also take their part, as women did in the early years of Islam. The valuable services rendered by women are recounted throughout history, from which we learn that women were not created solely for pleasure and comfort. From their examples we learn that we must all contribute toward the development of our nation, and that this cannot be done without being equipped with knowledge" (Benard, 2005).

ter Daoud Khan, and during that era, many women worked within the government as administrators, police, and military personnel.[7]

In present-day Afghanistan, inclusive governance structures have been mandated by outside organizations, have resulted from international pressure, and have been imposed via artificial mandates. The electoral quotas, included in the new Afghan constitution as it was drafted under the tutelage of the international community, are an example. This formal track of "decreeing" the development of women has had some successes.[8] Perhaps most notably, it has encountered an unexpected amount of grassroots resonance, with ordinary women and men not only seizing the opportunities inherent in the moment, but pushing forward with their own momentum. In the initial Loya Jirgas, for example, observers had initially expressed doubts that women would have the desire or the courage to attend, or that men would tolerate their presence. But not only did women attend, they also took especially bold stances against the reinstatement of warlords, nepotism, and corruption. In the 2003 Loya Jirga, for example, a 25-year-old woman named Malalai Joya took the floor to criticize the *mujahidin* as being responsible for the civil war that devastated the country and led to the Taliban takeover. She received multiple death threats but two years later was elected to parliament by the people of her province, Farah. Despite her youth, gender, and uncommonly outspoken manner, she was selected to head a delegation of tribal elders who wished to convince President Karzai that an ex-Taliban provincial governor ought to be replaced.[9]

The policies and strategies related to women's inclusion and gender equity in nation-building have at least three discrete dimensions: the role of official programs and state policies, second-track actions, and the impact of both streams of action on the unfolding nation-building effort. Discussion of these issues must consider the adversarial use of the gender issue by those who oppose the new post-conflict government.

---

[7] Azarbaijani-Moghadam, 2004, p. 97.

[8] For a case study of one such success, the National Solidarity Program, see Chapter Six.

[9] BBC News, "Profile: Malalai Joya," November 12, 2005, available at http://news.bbc.co.uk/go/pr/fr/-/2/hi/south_asia/4420832.stm (as of October 25, 2007).

In 1998, a "strategic framework" plan for Afghanistan was suggested by the United Nations. That plan foresaw a prioritization of the role of civil-society organizations, which was, of course, reflective of the circumstances prevailing at the time; under Taliban rule, no other course of action was possible. Today, second-track programs compensate for the national government's lack of resources and the absence of national reach. They address needs that the national government as yet is in no position to meet, and they maintain activities where the national government has no presence.[10]

Civil-society groups and the second-track approach generally include more women than are found in more-formal processes. Here, they take action "beneath the radar of the . . . traditional peace and security framework."[11] Creating and maintaining effective civil-society institutions is often difficult in post-conflict situations, where people "have difficulty creating formal organizations and asserting their legitimacy."[12]

There is quite a bit of positive evidence of women's inclusion in governance in Afghanistan since 2001. The transitional governments included several female ministers and saw the establishment of a Ministry of Women's Affairs to lend formal weight to the topic. As teachers and office administrators, women were well represented among the first waves of government hiring and were thus a visible part of the "face" of the new government. An equal-rights amendment and guarantees of parliamentary representation through legal quotas were included in the new constitution without much resistance from either the population at large or conservative groups such as the religious leadership; even the notoriously regressive head of the Supreme Court did not take issue with women's government employment or with these passages in the constitution. Women participated in every Loya Jirga and showed a good voter turnout; again, none of these things caused a public stir.

However, it is important not to confuse grassroots toleration with grassroots activism. In other words, while the bulk of the Afghan public

---

[10] Marshall, 2000.

[11] Woodrow Wilson International Center for Scholars, 2004a.

[12] Anderlini, Conaway, and Keys, 2004.

was apparently at peace with these innovations and even willing to participate in them, this should not be mistaken for an active demand. A small grassroots minority, by no means consisting only of women, shows active endorsement, while a larger majority appears to be adopting a wait-and-see attitude before coming to any judgment. This is not out of keeping with Afghanistan's political culture in general, which is accustomed to adapting itself to changes introduced from above and from the outside, reflecting a history of authoritarian rule, monarchs, frequent abrupt changes in values and governance, and steady attempts at conquest by outsiders.

As the transitional government moves toward greater permanence and stakeholders begin more overtly to assert themselves, the first erosions in the externally encouraged elevated role of women are appearing. Isobel Coleman of the Council on Foreign Relations observes that "women's inclusion in Afghanistan's government, which the international community has been using as an indicator of democratic progress, is actually regressing."[13]

Table 4.1 provides some substantiation for that claim. Women's roles in the presidential cabinet, for example, which is free of external management, have fallen away. Additionally, there are no women on the Afghan Supreme Court. Like the Supreme Court justices, the provincial governors are appointed by the president, and in one of the few positive developments, a woman is the governor of Bamiyan province.

Active participation by women in transitional and permanent decisionmaking institutions can substantially increase both the local and global security of a nation. Mary Caprioli found that both the percentage of women in decisionmaking bodies and the duration of women's inclusion in suffrage at the outset of a crisis can have statistically significant effects, lessening the duration of the violence at "national, transitional and international levels."[14]

In her chapter "Nation-Building Unraveled: Aid, Peace and Justice in Afghanistan," Sippi Azarbaijani-Moghadam explores the role of second-track NGO work within the post-conflict context: "The work

---

[13] Coleman and Hunt, 2006.

[14] Caprioli and Boyer, 2001. Also see Caprioli (2003).

Table 4.1
Ratios of Women in Political Positions in Afghanistan

Event	Cabinet Ministers	Provincial Governors	Supreme Court	Loya Jirga	
				Upper Meshrano Jirga	Lower Wolesi Jirga
2001–2003 Transitional Government (Afghan Interim Authority)					
Bonn Commission 2001				10 percent (6/60)	
Emergency Loya Jirga				12 percent (200/1650)	
Constitutional Drafting Commission	2/29			20 percent (2/9)	
Constitutional Review Commission				20 percent (7/35)	
Constitutional Loya Jirga				20 percent (105/500)	
2004					
Presidential elections	3/34	0	0		
2005					
Parliamentary elections	0/34	1/34	0	23	28 percent (68: quota +6)

of women's NGOs has evolved rapidly and they have moved into new areas dealing with more sensitive issues such as women rights protection and domestic violence. A number of Afghan women's NGOs have the grassroots contacts and professionalism to represent women's majority interests effectively."[15] Today, data regarding the NGOs' role in Afghanistan's reconstruction are incomplete, and many believe it is much too early in the process to really know the role of NGOs in this particular post-conflict setting.

---

[15] Azarbaijani-Moghadam, 2004, p. 111.

Second-Track Governance: Three Lessons from Post-Conflict Afghanistan

> True peace cannot be imposed from above, but must be built, nurtured and sustained from the bottom up. Much of this difficult work of building peace is carried out at the community level by grassroots organizations and women's organizations, organizations that represent those very sectors of society that are generally excluded from participation at the formal negotiation table.[16]
>
> — *Donna Ramsey Marshall*

This section discusses three reform cases in post-conflict Afghanistan: one highly successful case, one a medium success, and one that failed. Recommendations are drawn from the first two cases.

Elections

At a cost of $148 million from donor countries and the United Nations, the 2005 elections for Afghanistan's Wolesi Jirga (lower house) and 34 provincial councils held great stakes not only for women, but for the larger community as well. Twelve million Afghans over the age of 18 were qualified to vote, in a system in which all candidates were independent, i.e., did not run within a political party.[17]

By all accounts, these elections were a great success for the women of Afghanistan. With the lessons of the 2004 presidential election in mind, women's advocacy groups started early, identifying the problems and challenges the process was likely to create for women's participation both as voters and as candidates.[18] Table 4.1 lists some of the challenges faced, the solutions chosen, and their effects on the elections.

For the elections of 2005, government-supported and NGO-led programs conducted public information campaigns and other projects to encourage voter participation in general and female voter registration

---

[16] Marshall, 2000.

[17] BBC News, "Q&A: Afghan Election Guide," October 3, 2005, available at http://news.bbc.co.uk/1/hi/world/south_asia/4251580.stm (as of October 25, 2007).

[18] One of the greatest challenges to women's work in the 2004 election concerned security and personal safety. Effects of insurgent attacks on voting are discussed in Chapter Two.

Table 4.2
Women and the 2005 Afghan Parliamentary Election

Challenge	Solution	Results
Polling-station security	Polling centers were divided equally between male and female voters; 17 percent of international election observers and 38 percent of domestic observers were women.[a]	44 percent of new voters were women;[b] 43 percent of the electorate was women, up from 40 percent the year before (presidential election).
Political parties	Single non-transferable vote system (SNTV) placed candidates as individuals, not as party list members.	Capitalized on women's ability to not have prior political affiliation and thus "blood on their hands" from prior party acts; most women ran as independents.[c]
Candidates	12 percent of Wolesi Jirga candidates and 8 percent of provincial candidates were women.	28 percent of Wolesi Jirga seats held by women (6 more seats than the quota); only a combined total of 5 seats in 3 provinces will remain vacant because there were not enough female candidates.
Voter registration	Barriers for participation were kept low, and women were educated on their right to become involved.	Registration by women increased 35 percent in Uruzgan province and 23 percent in Helmand province.
Voter education	Initiatives to include voter education for women were vital at the rural level; education was often most effective if classes were separated by sex.	35 percent of the 1,844 voter educators were women; 2.4 million women received some sort of civic education and outreach.[a]
Institutionalization of efforts	Creation of the Joint Electoral Management Body (JEMB)	220 of 830 small grants given were to women's groups, which reached 58,475 women throughout the country; a media unit, created to ensure that voters had an opportunity to make an informed choice, was used by 77 percent of women candidates.[a]

[a] Joint Electoral Management Body, 2005.

[b] Anderlini, Conaway, and Keys, 2004.

[c] For more on political parties, see JEMBS (Joint Electoral Management Body Secretariat) database at http://www.afghan-web.com/politics/political_parties.pdf.

in particular. They also correctly identified physical safety and security as a major concern, prompted by several highly public acts of violence against women in the 2004 presidential-election cycle.[19] As they had in 2004, the NGOs created women-only voting stations staffed by female election workers and offered the highly publicized option of voter registration cards without the requirement of being photographed.

The NGOs involved in this effort were dynamic and diverse, and international groups partnered with Afghan organizations to implement the programs. For example, the UK-based NGO Womankind[20] paired with the Afghan Women's Network to help register thousands of women across the country. Starting in 2003, the two organizations created campaigns to involve women in voter education and civic engagement, focusing on provincial-level activities. These included finding women leaders to speak out on the importance of voting, sending them on speaking tours of the country, and conducting workshops on the role of women during the election period. With the Afghan Women's Education Center (AWEC), Womankind ran a program entitled "Peace and Democracy," which worked with women's centers across the country to provide a variety of local social services, including voter education. Attempts were also made to draw in male, religious, and conservative communities.

In a third partnership, with the Afghan Women's Resource Centre (AWRC), Womankind supported literacy training and civic education in Kabul, Parwan, and Kapisa provinces. About 600 women took part in approximately 20 training workshops.

The Constitution

NGOs played a role in the Afghan constitutional process, helping to shape both the procedural aspects and the final product. While this was partly mandated by the Bonn Process, which called for transpar-

---

[19] These acts included a June 2004 attack on a bus carrying female election workers, which resulted in the death of two women; the same month, a gunman attacked a bus carrying registered voters, brutally killing 16 people.

[20] For more information, see the group's web site, http://www.womankind.org.uk/vision-and-mission.html (as of October 25, 2007).

JOINT ELECTORAL MANAGEMENT BODY

The Joint Electoral Management Body (JEMB) was created under the auspices of its predecessor, the Interim Afghan Electoral Commission, and focused on assisting the institutionalization of the voting mechanism in Afghanistan. Four of its 13 members are women. In addition to carrying out the elections, the board is responsible for "establishing policy guidelines, approving procedures, and exercising oversight over the electoral process." The JEMB maintained a gender information unit and a web site. Within its small grants program, 220 of 830 small grants were given to women's groups for projects believed to have reached 58,475 women throughout the country. JEMB's media unit was used by 77 percent of the women candidates. The purpose of that program was to assist inexperienced candidates and those without independent resources to learn about constructing and running a political campaign. Overall, this program had 34 provincial offices where provincial election officers and regional election coordinators worked to "get the word out." Through active decentralization, progressive marketing, and inclusiveness, the JEMB took on many of the characteristics of successful NGOs. This created a bottom-up approach via formal institutional means, which garnered much success for the women of Afghanistan.

SOURCE: Joint Electoral Management Body, 2005.

---

ency and equity in the creating of a constitution, it was also a product of basic supply and demand, as portions of the process were outsourced to groups with relevant expertise.

In June 2000, in Tajikistan, NEGAR, a Paris-based NGO, held a conference that brought together 300 Afghan women from all over the world to create a document entitled "Declaration of the Essential Rights of Afghan Women," which was signed into law in 2003 by the interim administration of Afghanistan. The document, still in effect today, calls for "equity between men and women, equal protection under the law, institutional education in all disciplines, freedom of movement, freedom of speech and political participation and the right to wear or not wear a burqa or scarf."[21] This piece constituted a declaration of basic human rights for women, tenuring the foundation of

---

[21] Sultan, 2005, p. 7.

human rights within the constitution and introducing an institutionalized role for women in the process of its creation.

In preparation for the Constitutional Loya Jirga in 2003,[22] Women for Afghan Women[23] and the Afghan Women's Network[24] hosted a conference assembling 45 women in conservative Kandahar. The group drafted a Women's Bill of Rights, which was presented to then–Minister of Women's Affairs Habiba Sarabi at the Constitutional Commission of the Transitional Islamic State of Afghanistan. The document was endorsed by President Karzai and prompted him to declare that half of his appointed delegates to the Constitutional Loya Jirga would in fact be women.[25] This was seen as a significant validation of the group's work.[26]

The Afghan Civil Society Forum (ACSF) became especially influential during the time of the Constitutional Commission by engaging the public with information campaigns.[27] ACSF's focus on public awareness and education helped create momentum in the months leading up to the vote on the constitution.[28]

Despite these examples of effective NGO activity in relation to the constitution, we assess the constitutional process overall as only partly successful, because of the issue of implementation, which was

---

[22] For more information on the Constitutional Loya Jirga and the constitutional process, see Appendix B.

[23] The Women for Afghan Women mission statement says, "The inclusion of women in all decision-making processes is a requirement of a democratic society." Available at the Women for Afghan Women web site, http://www.womenforafghanwomen.org/ (as of October 25, 2007).

[24] The Afghan Women's Network mission statement calls for a "nonpartisan network of women and women's NGOs working to empower Afghan women and ensure their equal participation in Afghan society." Available at the Afghan Women's Network web site, http://www.afghanwomensnetwork.org/index.php?q=node/ (as of October 25, 2007).

[25] President Karzai was convinced that his reelection depended on the votes of women and was a strong supporter of campaigns to register them to vote. Survey results conducted by his staff confirmed his view (personal communication, spring 2004).

[26] Sultan, 2005, p. 13.

[27] Brunet and Helal, 2003, p. 14.

[28] Ibid.

scarcely addressed by any of the participant actors. There is a great disconnect between the abstract rights of the women of Afghanistan as written in the constitution and the actual, practical circumstances of their lives and daily treatment. Given the baseline of near-total disenfranchisement and oppression established by the Taliban and resting on a foundation of traditional backwardness, such a disconnect was inevitable. However—and all the more so because it was eminently foreseeable—more thought should have been given to the means by which these principles would be communicated to the population, including legal professionals, educators, and law-enforcement officials, and, however gradually, implemented. Lack of clarity in several key clauses was another problem; these clauses are cited in Table 4.3. While NGOs were able to participate in the constitution-writing process, exhaustion of resources may have kept them from doing meaningful follow-up work, such as education and media campaigns to clarify how these rights should be manifested in everyday life.

The high levels of engagement and effort that went into ensuring a contemporary, equitable outcome for women by the constitution stand in stark and surprising contrast to the absence of any serious planning for the realization of the constitution's lofty standards in real life. The widespread abuses suffered by Afghan women throughout their lifetimes, the absence of recourse, the pervasiveness of oppressive tribal customs, and the multiple wrongful applications of misunderstood Islamic law to the disadvantage of women were amply known. That the precepts of the constitution would not somehow magically trickle down and transform society could also have been predicted. A sustained process of education, with special attention to the judiciary and the police and with public-awareness campaigns to explain how these principles contribute to improved societal life, will be necessary but has not yet been undertaken.

Table 4.3
Key Clauses Pertaining to Women in the Afghan Constitution

Issue	Goal	Clause	Assessment
Legal representation	Giving women their "day in court."	Article 31: The state is obligated to appoint an attorney for the destitute.	There are not nearly enough state attorneys, nor do most women know that they have the right to be provided with one; people often go unrepresented.
Religious rights	Integrating Islamic Holy Law, while still allowing for the protection of human rights as mandated by international law.	Article 3: The Hanafi school of law was chosen for the country.[a]	Legal experts had recommended a code of law drawn from all of the Islamic schools of law.[b]
International law	Integrating international law and retaining its support of women.	Article 7: The state must recognize all internationally approved statements on human rights.	Many are unfamiliar with international law, and there are no enforcement mechanisms.
Minority and individual rights	Security for the rights of the person and minorities.	Article 58: Established an independent human-rights commission.	The commission lacks influence.
Women's rights	Legal equity.	Article 22: Men and women are equal under the law.	The constitution is not backed up by meaningful and applicable penal codes.
Equal representation under the law	Quota system.	Article 83: Women should hold one-third of the seats in the upper house (a 17 percent quota) and 25 percent of the seats in the lower house, or at least two seats from each province.	

[a]Additionally, Article 7 set forth this interpretation in the frame of international human-rights law: "The state shall observe the United Nations Charter, interstate agreements, as well as international treaties to which Afghanistan has joined, and the Universal Declaration of Human Rights."

[b] Thus, language in the constitution should always recognize not only the basic principles of Islam, but also the principles of democracy, pluralism, social justice, rule of law, and Afghanistan's international obligations." This is an example of such a recommendation, cited in Benard and Hachigian (2003).

Legal Rights

Afghanistan has long had a system of justice based on multiple parallel precepts and processes.[29] The Hanafi school's interpretation of Shari'a law, folk versions of what uneducated religious authorities took to be Shari'a law, tribal customs, and civil laws promulgated in the capital of Kabul were all applied in various ways by different sets of actors for different circumstances.[30] In Afghanistan, historical tribal organization has created a set of practices built on two main principles regarding women. The first is that they are subordinate to men in society; the second is that they are responsible for the honor of the family and the extended family. These long-standing cultural traditions often usurp any legal code that exists, even where people are aware of its existence. A number of the practices related to these tribal traditions are strongly detrimental to the rights and well-being of women, and more than a few stand in flagrant violation of human rights and/or orthodox Islamic law and values.

For example, the widespread Afghan practice of child marriage—often taking the form of marrying hypothetical future children to each other before they are even conceived or born—is completely un-Islamic. In this practice, good friends or neighbors make a pledge that if in the future they have children of opposite genders, the children would marry. In a related custom, it is taken for granted that a male cousin has the "first right of refusal" over his female cousins, cousin marriage being considered ideal. Besides the problem of mutual incompatibility, this in many instances has led to marriages with very large age differences between the parties. These age differences could go in either direction, and it is not unheard of for an adult woman to find herself being married off to a juvenile. In addition to tradition, the families' property interests often play a role in such arrangements. Another problematic tradition involves the use of girls or young women to arbitrate a dispute. In instances where one family or clan has committed

---

[29] For a discussion of Muslim family law in a modern context, see Woodrow Wilson International Center for Scholars (2005). For more on citizenry and identity in Middle Eastern nations, see Joseph (2000), Cunningham (2005), and Joseph (1996).

[30] Chamlou, 2004, p. 25.

an offense against another, the offending side will offer the other side a bride as part of the reparations. It is understood that this girl or woman will serve in a scapegoat role, suffering the anger and punishment of the offended side for the rest of her life. Unfortunately, these and other equally egregious practices are still exercised in Afghanistan today. The strategy of the international community has been to work at building a modern civil law code and legal and judiciary system, in the expectation that over time, this system would overlay the older traditional practices. A minority view has held that it is important to confront and actively delegitimize the negative practices of tribal and local tradition, for example, by making it known that these are forbidden in Islam.

The formal legal structure also lacks fundamental provisions for property ownership and family law, which are vital for everyone and essential to the rebuilding effort, but which have additional impact on women, whose weaker position in society makes them more vulnerable to having their rights violated. The legal structure in regard to marriage, divorce, child custody, and other family-related matters is underdeveloped, which leaves these issues to the arbitrary regulation of families, clans, and tribes. It is important to put a cohesive legal structure in place, with a counseling component and at least some provision for social services to cushion the impact of change and protect the victims. Otherwise, there is a risk of what could be referred to as the "Hungary effect," where justice-seeking members of civil society are prematurely urged by outside agents to claim their rights but are not supported against the violence with which their effort is met.[31] Pakistan, where a campaign urging women to report domestic violence and incidents of honor crimes did not have any supporting mechanisms in place, is an example of this situation.[32] A rise in the incidence of violence followed the campaign, as reactionary forces tried to intimidate women against challenging the status quo.

---

[31] In 1956, the Hungarian populace rose up against Soviet dominance. The uprising initially appeared to be successful but was soon crushed by military intervention. U.S. public diplomacy, operating through Radio Free Europe, was later accused of raising false hopes about Western support for the uprising, thereby encouraging Hungarian civilians to take excessive risks and ultimately go to their doom.

[32] Amnesty International, 1999a.

Mohammad Rasa, Afghanistan's Interior Ministry spokesman, believes that there is a problem of "weak prosecution of perpetrators and a lack of awareness among women about their rights as the key factors driving the practice."[33] The solution, he believes, will require basic changes in behavior that has long been considered acceptable in Afghanistan.[34] One of the most distressing responses to this "behavior" is the high rate of female suicide. In 2005, the Afghan Independent Human Rights Commission documented 154 cases of self-immolation by women in the western part of the country alone. The commission noted that the actual rates are likely to be much higher, as many cases go unreported or misreported as accidents. The commission also believes that about 80 percent of these suicides are attributed to family violence. In some cases, it is also unclear whether the immolation occurred at the hands of family members or was done by the women themselves. "The increased reports of women and girls attempting to and taking their own lives in such a painful manner indicates an immense pressure and inability to cope with the oppression and violence in their lives."[35]

It seems probable that rising expectations of improved rights, when not realized, are the driving force behind the elevated number of suicide attempts—another instance of the "Hungary effect."

Violence against women is often treated as a private matter by the police, so these cases are not generally investigated or prosecuted properly.[36] Human-rights organizations such as Amnesty International point out that to reverse the trend in female deaths, "the responsibility lies with the state to exercise due diligence in holding private individuals such as family members punishable for abuses committed and resulting in desperate action by victims."[37] However, this would require a much stronger judicial system than currently exists, and it also presupposes a broad-based education campaign to change mindsets.

---

[33] United Nations Office for the Coordination of Humanitarian Affairs, 2006.

[34] Ibid.

[35] Ibid.

[36] Ibid.

[37] Ibid.

The failure to establish a consistent and effective rule-of-law regime and the consequences of that failure for women fall into several categories: national/public, national/private, and subnational/private. The first category consists of formal, secular legal codes, some of them long-standing, others newly created, that do not adequately address women's status and rights. The second category consists of legal codes, including those meant to protect women, which have not been implemented. The third category consists of the informal judicial structures and ideals of society that simply exist.[38] This situation applies not only to Afghanistan, but to many other countries in the developing world. NGOs tend to focus on the first category in an effort to bring law codes into better conformity with international standards of human and women's rights. This has been done with some success, for example, in sub-Saharan Africa, where institutional reform focused on constitutional law, commercial law, and civil law concerning land tenure, property ownership, and family and customary law.[39]

In Afghanistan, there are several examples of gaps and lapses within the first category. The 1971 Afghanistan Law of Marriage fails to define the age of marriage or to ban the practice of forced marriage. Similarly, the 1976 penal code, currently used as local law in Afghanistan, has no provisions against domestic violence. Both of these law codes allow prosecution under *zina*, which punishes women for engaging in sexual activities outside of marriage. According to some estimates, nearly 80 percent of the women in prison are there on convictions of *zina* crimes.[40] Such convictions, which often rest on the slender evidence of allegations, are known to be an easy way for a husband or family to rid itself of a woman who is inconvenient for entirely other reasons.

Development of the courts and the judicial process in Afghanistan has been spotty at best. Representatives of armed groups have in many cases been able to insert themselves into the court system as

---

[38] For a more complete illustration of Islamic family law, see Woodrow Wilson International Center for Scholars (2005).

[39] World Bank Group, 2000.

[40] Coleman and Hunt, 2006.

an extension of their respective warlords' powers. Even under the best of circumstances, women often feel that they can approach the male-dominated courts only through a male relative; otherwise, they risk denunciation for a lack of modesty and piety.

The following legal issues in Afghanistan are also cited by observers:

- Inmates are detained without charges.
- Those arrested are tried without representation.
- There is no adequate provision for family courts.
- Lawyers sanctioned by the Ministry of Women's Affairs (MOWA) do not have knowledge of the legal rights of women.
- Pretrial detainees are held with convicted offenders.
- Prisons are overcrowded, poorly sanitized, lacking food and water, and filled with the young children of inmates.[41]
- Criminals are released because of lack of prison space.
- There is a high rate of sexual abuse of inmates by police and prison officials.
- Women's prisons serve double duty as shelters for endangered women or women already victimized by crimes such as rape or attempted murder.

Prisons are also used to punish and break the will of women who are showing too much independence—refusing to return to an abusive husband, rejecting a marriage candidate selected by their family, refusing to separate from a fiancé the family disapproves of, and the like. It is estimated that as much as 70 to 80 percent of legal and quasi-legal activity is being applied informally via local Shura Councils or individual mullahs instead of by formal national courts and secular legal systems.

The creation of a state program similar to the JEMB could be beneficial. By decentralizing the issue, it could bring an information and implementation strategy to local provinces. Replicating the successful JEMB model, an official program could adopt a more NGO-

---

[41] Benard et al., 2003.

like approach and make substantial changes from the bottom up. In 2005, the Afghanistan Rule of Law Project, a USAID subsidiary, made some initial inroads into understanding the baseline legal practices of Afghanistan when it conducted 29 focus groups and 60 interviews across rural parts of the country. Participants included judges, mullahs, government leaders, police officers, law-school faculty, and activists. The resultant recommendations centered on the importance of information, civic-awareness campaigns, and institutional reform. Unfortunately, follow-on action has been sketchy.[42]

Prior to the national elections, the Afghan population was unfamiliar with most of the basic notions of democracy and voting; Afghan women had lived in enforced seclusion and *de facto* house arrest; the Taliban worldview, proclaiming it wrong for women to take part in public life on any level, had predominated. In awareness of these obstacles, as well as the logistical and cultural obstacles in the country, a combination of information, education, training, and accommodation created a successful outcome. A similar approach suggests itself for the domain of law. Training or retraining of lawyers and judges, information programs for police, and public-awareness campaigns should be conducted in parallel with the physical building of courts and prisons, which is currently ongoing. Media campaigns utilizing television, plays, and radio, as well as street theater, could be a helpful part of this.[43] Educating both girls and boys in provincial schools at an early age about the rule of law and about women's legal rights would also be effective, and there is a role for mullahs and religious leaders in clarifying the un-Islamic nature of many tribal customs.

Recommendations

Afghan women have demonstrated their determination to be part of the political reform process and the work of building their nation. Progress has been significant, even in areas where much less was expected, but

---

[42] United States Agency for International Development, 2005a.

[43] Afghanistan Research and Evaluation Unit, 2005.

careful consideration needs to be applied to two areas in particular: (1) sustainability in the face of renewed Taliban attacks and/or in light of a winding down of some of the international presence and resources, and (2) improved and enduring support for reforms achieved at elevated levels of the political system but needing to be rooted in the actual life of the society. The disconnect between the new direction as it is written and the way in which it is or is not understood and practiced remains vast. Groups must work to assess this disconnect, creating realistic and flexible mid- and long-term plans to begin bridging it. Failure to do so threatens to nullify much of what has been accomplished at the higher level.

Men are a critical part of that effort. Groups need to inform, and men and boys need to be informed and educated about intended changes to gender relations in society. They also need to understand the rationale and to see how this will improve the life of the whole society. Again, the national elections are a good precedent; Afghan men could have prevented women from participating in the voting, but have chosen not to.[44]

Replicating their approach in the 2005 elections, women's NGOs should focus on identifying the challenges that are logistically problematic for women in everyday life, especially in respect to their legal rights. First, they should consider overhauling the legal code, making key changes in the way in which the laws are written and understood. This will include making sure that all constitutional code is present and clear in penal and civil code and that it minimizes room for misinterpretation by local judicial systems. In addition, the rights and needs of women should be more absolutely defined, leaving as little room as possible for local-level "interpretation." A national court system is needed to control the interpretation of the general laws of the constitution. Particularly in rural areas, where "poverty curbs everyone's freedoms,"[45] laws and rights must be well-defined. Clarity would require research on what long-standing laws still have relevancy and applica-

---

[44] Benard et al., 2003.

[45] Interviews with Cory Ipp and Kathleen Lopez-Kim, June 10, 2003, in Benard et al., 2003.

bility and an assessment of how all laws fit in with a broader under-standing of international human-rights codes. Using the model that placed women in leadership positions for polling-station management and voter observation, women's groups should continually work at the critical task of placing women in judicial and legal positions, includ-ing as judges (at the national and the provincial level), attorneys, and advocates, not only to inform the content of the proceedings, but as a visible presence to encourage other women to find these institutions approachable. Additionally, women's groups should work hard to con-tinue engaging the interest of the international community, utilizing experts and long-standing rights groups to make recommendations for institutionalizing women's legal rights.[46]

---

[46] Anderlini, Conaway, and Keys, 2004.

CHAPTER FIVE

Economic Participation and Women

Introduction

The economy of Afghanistan has "probably done more to modify male-female relations than all the human rights rhetoric of the past fifty years or more."[1] In the post-conflict context, the reestablishment of a viable economic system presents both challenges and opportunities to nation-builders. By understanding women's complex long-term roles within the economic system, it is possible to support culturally salient best practices for guiding this relationship in the future.

Any effort to assess female participation in the Afghan economy, either now or during the Taliban period, must be viewed with skepticism. The structure of the economy and women's roles in it make accurate measurements or even good estimates extremely difficult. In this poverty-stricken country, a large proportion of what economic growth there is has long been driven by the illegal trade in drugs, while the gray and white economies are dependent to a large extent on a variety of income-generating activities for women, including crafts, services, and agricultural work, which are also difficult to measure accurately. Urban employment and participation in the shadow and black economies may be somewhat more measurable, but Afghanistan is predominantly rural. Women unquestionably play large roles related not only to their traditional responsibilities in households, but also to the disappearance of men from the social and economic scene due to years of conflict. Women also have a small but real presence in the paid work-

---

[1] Nancy Hatch Dupree, 2002 interview, in Azarbaijani-Moghaddam, 2004.

force, but it is very difficult to quantify that role, as women's work is not always or fully monetized and may occur under the radar of traditional economic analysis.[2]

That said, the question of female participation in the economy is crucial for the very reasons that it is difficult to measure. Women have always played a significant, if not always readily visible, economic role in Afghanistan, and this has increased, not decreased, over the years of conflict.[3] The revitalization and resurgence of Afghanistan's economy will therefore substantially depend on women's economic activity. Moreover, because men dominate the narcotics trade, the development of more traditionally female economic sectors can help ameliorate a family's dependence on narcotics production and trade.

Evaluating both the steady state and future development requires not simply data collection, but an improved understanding of what data to collect. Economic participation in Afghanistan must, for one thing, be measured differently than it is in more-developed, and more-peaceful, countries. Afghanistan also presents the many challenges of collecting data in post-conflict settings, where security and travel issues may trump the interest in getting good data. This chapter examines the available qualitative and quantitative information regarding women and girls' economic participation in Afghanistan and then presents some thoughts on implications for policies and programs.

Women and Afghanistan's Economy Before the War

According to the UNDP Human Development Report for Afghanistan (2004b), women played a significant role in Afghanistan's economy during the 1980s, comprising 70 percent of the country's teachers, 40 percent of its doctors, and half of its government workers.[4]

---

[2] *Gender Disparities as a Challenge to Human Development*, 2004.

[3] United Nations Economic and Social Council, 2001.

[4] Study on "Human Security and Livelihoods of Rural Afghans, 2002–2003," in United Nations Development Programme, 2004b.

At the same time, these numbers paint a somewhat misleading picture of Afghan society as a whole. Women (and men) working in these kinds of salaried jobs were an urban phenomenon in a rural country. Education and health care, too, were largely limited to urban areas. Dupree estimates that only about 3 percent of Afghanistan's school-age girls actually attended school during the 1980s, and most of these girls lived in cities, particularly in Kabul.[5]

This does not mean that women did not participate in the economy in rural areas, only that this economic activity is difficult to quantify. For example, agriculture is only one component of the rural economy, and a variety of other income-generating work was performed by women. Rural society in prewar Afghanistan was tightly kin-based, with a broad division of labor. Women had roles in household financial management, made contributions to agricultural tasks, and were responsible for a variety of work in the home, including child care and cooking, that were not directly financially remunerated, although the women did share in overall family wealth (not necessarily equitably). Typically, women were responsible for harvesting certain crops, such as beans and cotton; for domestic food-supply management; and for determining how much of the harvest was to be kept for the family and how much could be sold. Paid work by women was limited. Women traditionally have been the makers of Afghanistan's famous rugs, as well as a variety of other handicrafts; men did not participate in this work, which is generally grueling and poorly paid. Both men and women, however, traditionally collected the wool for the rugs. It is important to note that for work such as wool-gathering, in which men and women perform similar tasks, women reportedly were paid less than men.[6] Thus, we surmise that women in prewar Afghanistan were highly involved in a variety of economic activity but that most of it was not directly remunerated financially, and that when they did carry out paid work, they were likely to receive less money for it than were men doing the same or similar tasks. The limited available data support

---

[5] Dupree, 1998.

[6] United Nations Development Programme, 2004a,b; interview with Afghanistan government officials, March 2006; Barakat and Wardell, 2002.

these assumptions. The World Bank's World Development Indicators estimate that from 1990 to 1994, women made up about 34 percent of the workforce (defined as excluding homemakers and informal-sector workers but including the unemployed if they were seeking work). They also estimate that throughout that period and into the present, some 48 to 50 percent[7] of the working-age women worked in the labor force thus defined (compared with some 86 to 88 percent[8] of the men). The World Bank assesses that throughout this period, the balance of women (that is, the other half) were employed in the informal sector. Both the extrapolations and the simple subtraction make this assessment somewhat suspect, but it is interesting nonetheless. The bank further calculates, although only for 1990, the female participation rates in various economic areas. According to this dataset, 84.5 percent of employed Afghan women would have been employed in agriculture in 1990, compared with 63 percent of the men. Although women made up only 17.8 percent of the workers in the nonagricultural sectors, they did have roles. It is estimated that 12.9 percent of the working women worked in industry (compared with 9.5 percent of the working men). Women appear to have been excluded from service occupations: Only 2.6 percent of the 49 percent of women who worked were employed in that sector, compared with 27.5 percent of the men. This small number should, in principle, include female teachers.[9] Notably, the Population Reference Bureau estimated that women comprised 5 percent of Afghanistan's nonfarm wage earners in 1990.[10]

All of these numbers must be considered suspect and notional, of course, but they do reflect some knowledgeable assessments of women's situation in Afghanistan before the war.

---

[7] Increasing over time.

[8] Decreasing over time.

[9] World Bank, World Development Indicators Database, accessed in summer 2006. These data were not replicated in the database when it was accessed in February 2007.

[10] Population Reference Bureau, available at http://www.prb.org, accessed in February 2007.

Women and Afghanistan's Economy During the War and Under the Taliban

The war years affected women's participation in the economy in a number of ways. First, the overt economic role of women expanded. As men left their homes to become fighters, some never to return, women became *de facto* heads of households and took on greater economic and social roles, including land and property management and other agricultural activities.[11]

Although some rural women reportedly were forced into begging and prostitution,[12] many retained their traditional roles. The Afghanistan National Human Development Report (2004a) notes that women's economic contributions in Afghanistan continued (and continue) to include "food stock management, seed multiplication, animal husbandry, veterinarian and income generation via carpet-weaving in the rural areas . . . [and the contributions of] professional urban women."[13]

Solid data for the war years, however, are even more limited than for the pre-conflict period. Thus, while we have anecdotal descriptions of these changes, we have little in the way of quantitative information. We do know, however, that as the Taliban's power spread through Afghanistan, women's ability to hold jobs outside the home decreased. The Taliban issued a series of decrees prohibiting women from working outside the home, ostensibly for their protection. A July 2000 decree banned Afghan women from seeking or holding jobs in aid agencies, except in the health-care sector. In May 2001, another decree banned females from driving cars. Even foreign female Muslims in Afghanistan were required to be accompanied by male escorts. Those Afghan women who continued to work with the assistance community did so in the face of harassment and the threat of attack.[14]

---

[11] "Human Security and Livelihoods of Rural Afghans, 2002–2003," in United Nations Development Programme, 2004b.

[12] Barakat and Wardell, 2002.

[13] United Nations Development Programme, 2004a, citing Dupree, 1998, p. 7.

[14] United Nations, 2002.

Taliban decrees affected urban areas primarily and varied across the country, spreading as the regime consolidated its power. In Balkh, Mazar-e Sharif, Bamiyan, and Herat, schools continued to operate and women continued to go to work, including in the local government and aid agencies. In fact, after the Taliban took Kabul in 1994, female professors exiled from the capital set up a university in Bamiyan. However, as the Taliban pushed through the country, these freedoms faded.[15] It is worth noting that this primarily impacted a fairly small and urban proportion of women; life in the countryside did not change as significantly. A survey by Physicians for Human Rights published in August 2001 of small numbers (about 200 each) of women heads of household in Taliban-controlled and non–Taliban-controlled areas found that the vast majority of these women, 82 percent in the Taliban areas and 89 percent in the non-Taliban areas, reported their profession as home-maker.[16] It would be reasonable to estimate, however, that many of these women were involved in informal-sector work of some sort to keep their families fed and alive. According to Dupree, women working outside the home in rural Afghanistan under the Taliban tended to work in family groups and achieved "status and a sense of personal fulfillment . . . through motherhood, the creativity of handiwork and efficient household management."[17] This describes, of course, a situation similar to rural life in Afghanistan before the war. Moreover, it is worth noting that the questions asked affected the data. Women in Afghanistan are unlikely to describe themselves as "tradesmen" when asked for their occupation. They may, however, report that they create and sell products such as handicrafts.

Thus, our knowledge of the actual impact of the Taliban on women's economic role remains imprecise. However, we do know that Taliban rules were noticed and perceived as restrictive, with some unexpected results. For example, some argue that the bans on the schooling of girls gave rise to the growth of underground schools and helped foster

---

[15] International Crisis Group, 2003.

[16] Amowitz et al., 2001.

[17] Dupree, 1998.

the development of educational NGOs that continue to operate.[18] This silver lining, however, was insufficient to make up for the devastating ironies of Taliban-controlled Afghanistan, where the combination of restricted economic participation for women and the shrunken numbers of men after years of warfare meant that the difficulty of providing for a family increased. Women had to take on the traditionally male role of head of the family, while lacking the education and opportunity to work.[19] In the 1970s, just over 1 percent of Afghanistan's households were headed by women. By 1996, there were reportedly 45,000 war widows in Kabul alone, each supporting an average of six persons in her household.[20]

Women and Afghanistan's Economy Today

The situation for women in Afghanistan today remains complex, reflecting the damage done by years of conflict. Forcing the Taliban from power did not alleviate many of the economic problems faced by Afghanistan's population. While women are no longer precluded by national law from working outside the home, they continue to face a variety of significant constraints. According to the Afghanistan National Human Development Report, "Poverty dis-empowers Afghan women much more insidiously than official discrimination does. As long as women are focused on meeting their own and their families' basic needs for food, water, and shelter, they are effectively blocked from seeking real power via education, activism, and legislation."[21]

As elsewhere in South Asia, poverty is what drives most of Afghanistan's working women to work for wages. Afghans see women working for pay as an indicator, in and of itself, of household poverty.[22] Regretta-

---

[18] International Crisis Group, 2003.

[19] Ibid.

[20] World Bank, 2005.

[21] United Nations Development Programme, 2004a.

[22] Schutte, 2006

bly, the same social constraints that make women working an anomaly also create conditions in which these women are less able to monetize their economic activity than are men, ensuring that poverty endures. While the data are imprecise (and estimates are somewhat suspect, as noted elsewhere in this chapter), there is no question that women earn far less than men do for similar work (perhaps less than half) and that they face a number of structural challenges in their efforts to provide for their families.[23]

Gender division often occurs according to the product of the task. Rural women work in orchards, in melon fields, and in vegetable plots; few work in the wheat fields. Women prepare the soil for seeding, they weed, they plant, and they process foods after harvest, cleaning and drying vegetables, fruits, and nuts.

Some tasks are differentiated by age, with older women reportedly more likely to migrate with livestock than are younger women, who in turn are more likely to be involved in carpet weaving. Women also take care of household livestock, and some rural women raise chickens. The World Bank reports that women's roles in livestock production and dairy processing are increasing, although most of their labor remains nonmonetized.[24]

Wealth as well as gender determines women's roles. Wealthier women are more likely than poor women to be involved in embroidery and tailoring.[25] Although with some regional variation, they are less likely to work visibly on the land. But need can overcome social stigmas, and labor-intensive crops bring women as well as men into the fields.[26] Conversely, it is reported that some unemployed men have taken on carpet weaving and other traditionally female tasks.[27]

---

[23] World Bank, 2005.

[24] Ibid.

[25] Ibid.

[26] Grace, 2004; World Bank, 2005.

[27] Schutte, 2006.

Why aren't women paid for their work in the fields?[28] The reasons for this lie in social stigmas attached not just to working, but to traveling and interacting with others, stigmas that are particularly strong in the countryside. Women are not involved in the sale of goods at the bazaar, where such activities take place. Except for some childless widows, rural women are confined to their village environment. This cuts them off not only from direct earning capacity, but also from financial decisions, for though they may have a role in making those decisions in some households, it is the men who have the final authority.[29]

Some women's traditional activities do involve creating goods for sale, including knotted carpets, woven carpets (*gilims*), hats, and embroidery, as was the case before and during the war. These activities are not stigmatized, as they have a long historical precedent. But they are also difficult to leverage into economic power, primarily because of the restrictions on women's mobility.

Lack of mobility is one of the most important factors in Afghanistan women's inability to attain more economic power. Rural Afghan women who produce products for sale do not sell these products themselves, because social mores, if not national legislation, preclude them from traveling to the bazaars. Thus, they are dependent on male family members or wholesalers or other middlemen. Sometimes women work on commission and/or receive wool from suppliers, who also then sell the finished product. These are prevalent activities, and in large households, younger women concentrate on weaving, due to their better eyesight and strength, while older women are engaged in housework and the care of children. However, they are very poorly paid and their exclusion from market roles ensures that they get only a very small portion of the final sale price. Thus, little actual income is generated from these activities, and goods are sometimes bartered rather than sold.[30]

---

[28] One could argue that insofar as these are family businesses, men also aren't "paid" for their work. Men, however, manage and spend money. Women do not.

[29] Grace, 2004.

[30] Grace, 2004; World Bank, 2005; Schutte, 2006.

Taken in sum, all of this "traditional" female economic activity, paid or bartered, is probably more valuable than it may seem. In Afghanistan's highly informal economy, with 80 to 90 percent of activity estimated to be in the black or gray economies, barter and non-monetized work become very important. And, although women are precluded from selling products at market, they are able to trade items such as handicrafts or the eggs from their chickens in their villages.[31] However, this sort of value, while contributing to Afghanistan's overall economy, does not contribute proportionately to the required effort to the benefit of the women themselves or their households.

Property ownership is another area where laws may not discriminate against women, but practice and tradition prevent women from taking full advantage of their rights. Afghan secular law and Shari'a law both allow for female property inheritance and ownership. However, the reality is that few women in Afghanistan inherit or own property. The situation varies by ethnic group and region, however, with Tajik women more likely to inherit land than their Uzbek or Pashtun compatriots. In general, women's lack of education and weak social position make it relatively easy to deprive them of their ownership rights. Additionally, the traditional view posits it as somehow disadvantageous for women to exercise their rights to land ownership and puts pressure on them to cede these rights to husbands or male relatives.[32] Thus, women may live on land that might even be legally theirs, but they do not enjoy the rights and benefits of owning that land. The exceptions to this rule are widows, who are more likely to be perceived as owning land, although they are generally still precluded from selling it (a right that passes to sons or other male relatives).[33] Women also usually lack ownership rights or access to equipment and materials.[34]

Educated and trained women face a somewhat different set of circumstances. The opportunities that opened to women after the Tal-

---

[31] Grace, 2004; Wakefield, 2005.

[32] World Bank, 2005.

[33] Grace, 2004.

[34] World Bank, 2005.

iban fell were primarily urban and benefited educated women (a tiny group) disproportionately. After years of limiting women's access to education and opportunity, Afghanistan lacks qualified female workers, and there is a tremendous need for them. Fields that were not traditionally open to women, as well as those that have been, are in great need of competent personnel. For example, shortly after the Taliban were expelled, the Ministry of Education reported a shortage of 28,000 teachers. Moreover, many of the existing teachers are underqualified. Although there is also a shortage of male teachers (about one-third of Afghanistan's teachers today are women), more women are needed if, for example, girls' schools are to function (in Kabul, female teachers do outnumber male teachers). Of course, pay rates for teachers also remain low, exacerbating the problem, as qualified teachers seek better-paying work, for example, with foreign NGOs.[35]

Educated women, particularly those with English-language skills, are likely to find employment without much difficulty in Kabul. Although many of the jobs they can find, such as teaching and nursing, are quite poorly paid, they do provide options.[36] But again, those options are in the city—rural female doctors have reportedly been leaving their communities, seeking better-paying jobs in cities. Moreover, discrimination remains a factor. Cultural acceptance is one aspect of this, but legal and governmental restrictions also remain at all levels and in all sectors. Female judges in Afghanistan are rare outside of Kabul. With the exception of those responsible for juvenile and family courts, women judges are generally employed functionally as clerks, not as adjudicators.[37]

Urban employment includes a range of activities. For women without education, jobs in Kabul are limited to housework—cleaning, ironing, and laundering.[38] This situation is exacerbated by the lack

---

[35] "Human Security and Livelihoods of Rural Afghans, 2002–2003," in United Nations Development Programme, 2004b; World Bank, 2005.

[36] Danish Immigration Service, 2002.

[37] Amnesty International, 2004a.

[38] Danish Immigration Service, 2002.

of child-care options for poor women.[39] Efforts to provide daycare in Afghanistan are generally centered on government structures such as ministries, where they again reach the better-educated and wealthier members of society, not the vast majority of the Afghan public.[40]

Urban women are primarily involved in services and production, very rarely in trade. There are women entrepreneurs, most of whom work out of their homes and perhaps do not view their work as a real "business"—these include hairdressers and seamstresses. However, many self-employed women (almost half of them) report that they control their own income.[41]

In some regions, the situation is worse than in others. In Herat, for example, there continue to be reports of significant restrictions on women's economic participation. While women may now leave their homes without a male chaperone, they are still not allowed to walk or ride in a car with a man who is not a relative, which significantly diminishes their capacity for movement (for instance, they cannot ride in a taxi). Failure to wear a burqa in public is grounds for harassment, including by local police. There are also limitations on the jobs women may take. Local governor Ismail Khan has reportedly pressured women not to take jobs with NGOs or international organizations, yet very few government jobs have been opened to them. In fact, the local government has stated its intent to segregate government offices by gender. Women who have sought driver's licenses in Herat to increase their ability to get around and thus contribute to the economy have been refused. Women with licenses have had them confiscated. Thus, women in Herat are limited to work they can do in the home or near it.[42]

Although there are many reports of begging, prostitution, and child labor among Afghan women and children impoverished by the

---

[39] World Bank, 2005.

[40] Womankind Worldwide, 2002.

[41] World Bank, 2005.

[42] Human Rights Watch, 2002a.

war,[43] there is conflicting evidence on whether or not women have turned to increased involvement in the country's huge drug trade. Reports from neighboring states, such as Kyrgyzstan, Turkmenistan, and Tajikistan, through which the drug trade flows, suggest increasing rates of female involvement, particularly as traffickers. This is consistent with global data on increased illegal activities by women heads of household in post-conflict societies. The evidence in Afghanistan is mixed, however. Along with reports of female involvement in the drug trade, there are also reports that women do not take part in this business. One analyst who traveled extensively through Afghanistan doing research on the drug business there reported that he saw no evidence of women being involved as growers, dealers, or couriers.[44] The World Bank reports that female involvement in opium production is increasing, along with the trade, but that it is regionalized: Those in the south are not involved in poppy cultivation (although they may prepare food and drink for the men who are), while elsewhere in the country, women are involved in the full range of opium planting, harvesting, and processing. Moreover, the report notes that women's role in opium production "is more visible and more valued" than their role in wheat production, and women in Badakshan, at least, are at times paid for this work.[45]

Thus, the bottom line is that except in health and education, women's employment in Afghanistan does not look very different from their historical situation or from the state of affairs in other South Asian countries.[46] Most women work outside the home because of severe poverty and see working as a sign thereof. They have little hope of using work to break out of that poverty, however, because the work available to them pays little and because they continue to be highly marginal-

---

[43] Barakat and Wardell, 2001.

[44] International Crisis Group (2003) citing Anwer (2001), which reports women and children among refugees imprisoned for involvement in the drug trade and states that these women and children lost men in the war and were seeking to provide for their families (personal communication with a Kyrgyzstan-based analyst, March 2006).

[45] World Bank, 2005.

[46] Ibid.

ized in political and economic decisionmaking. The lack of mobility or capacity to engage in trade directly further hampers women's capacity to attain economic self-sufficiency.[47] It can also limit the capacity of the household as a whole, whether or not the woman works: An ill female must be accompanied by a male family member to medical appointments, for example, keeping the man, too, out of the workplace. Finally, socially acceptable income-generating activities such as carpet-weaving generally involve very young girls, raising child labor issues as well.[48]

The difference from other South Asian countries and from Afghanistan's history is that while women may do much the same work as men, Afghanistan's success and its people are more dependent on that work—and thus are more directly hurt by women's poor economic standing. Current estimates of the proportion of female-headed households vary considerably by locality, but they are much higher than in the past, with the lowest estimates for some areas at 4 percent of households and the highest rising to 20 percent.[49]

Assistance and Impact

This situation raises a number of questions for policy. The international donor community has viewed the empowerment and increased participation of women as a goal and has implemented a number of programs to achieve that goal. USAID's strategic plan for Afghanistan, for example, clearly identifies goals such as helping women to "enhance their social and economic well being." The plan asserts that gender equity is built into every aspect of its programs.[50] The World Bank and

---

[47] Schutte, 2006.

[48] Ibid.

[49] World Bank, 2005.

[50] United States Agency for International Development, 2005, available at http://www.usaid.gov/locations/asia_near_east/countries/afghanistan/ (as of October 25, 2007).

a number of other organizations also have gender components in their Afghanistan assistance.[51]

Current efforts are geared toward building on the activities women are already involved in. Financing small businesses of the sort that women can operate from their homes or collectively through women's centers is one aspect of this. Existing local funding options are limited and sometimes counterproductive. For example, the carpet weavers of the north, who obtain funding from those who sell their carpets in the market, receive the funds at such high rates of interest that their profit is minimal.[52] To provide alternatives and ensure that a broader range of Afghanistan's citizens have access to loans, the World Bank is helping finance the First Microfinance Bank of Afghanistan, which provides access to financing for micro and small businesses to stimulate economic growth and incomes. The bank's Afghanistan Reconstruction Trust Fund includes the Microfinance Support for Poverty Reduction Project, the goal of which is to help Afghanistan develop a microfinance sector to provide poor people with financial services and help "remove the barriers that separate the microfinance community from the broader mainstream financial system." The project has provided over $28 million and is working with 12 microfinance institutions. It supports a network of 128 branches, with more than 119,000 clients in 17 provinces and 120 districts. The World Bank reports that 85 percent of the program's clients are women, and repayment is approximately 99 percent. It employs 1,500 Afghans, two-thirds of them women.[53] Similarly, USAID states that of the 28,000 loans the U.S. government provided to small businesses in Afghanistan, 75 percent were to women. The loans are being used for training in areas such as bee-keeping, poultry farming, kitchen gardens, and home-based dairy production.

---

[51] U.S. Department of State, 2005.

[52] "Human Security and Livelihoods of Rural Afghans, 2002–2003," in United Nations Development Programme, 2004b.

[53] "The World Bank in Afghanistan: Country Update," January 2006, www.worldbank. org/af (as of October 25, 2007).

USAID also funds handicraft programs and is planning to assist in creating a handicraft marketing and training center.[54]

Critics, however, argue that donors do not have a sufficient understanding of gender issues, and thus their programs fail to improve women's situation. The Afghanistan Research and Evaluation Unit notes that "most agricultural programs do not have an explicit gender equity agenda."[55] In another report, the unit notes that there exists among donors "no coherent single gender policy at the macro or micro level."[56] It also notes that NGOs working in Afghanistan continue to operate in an emergency-relief framework, rather than a development one—thus, they seek to implement high-impact and immediate-impact projects, rather than seeking to create long-term sustainable change.[57] Womankind Worldwide has also expressed concern about the long-term sustainability, lasting support, and longer-term effectiveness of economic programs in Afghanistan.[58]

It is difficult to assess the impact of the efforts that are under way. Data on the microcredit loans programs, for example, tend to focus on how many loans are granted and how many are repaid. This does not, however, necessarily provide useful information on the impact of the loans.[59] Global experience suggests that microcredit efforts are most effective when they are combined with some sort of training, which suggests that many of the World Bank and USAID projects are on the right track, but it is not clear that the bulk of the aid provides training—or that the training is useful or efficient, or that it meets the needs of local women and men. According to a March 2003 Inter-

---

[54] "Afghanistan: International Women's Day Special Report," March 8, 2006, http://www. usaid.gov/locations/asia_near_east/countries/afghanistan/index.html (as of October 25, 2007).

[55] Grace, 2004.

[56] Afghanistan Research and Evaluation Unit, 2005.

[57] Afghanistan Research and Evaluation Unit, 2005.

[58] Womankind Worldwide, 2002, available at http://www.womankind.org.uk/cgi-bin/htsearch?words=Taking+Stock&method=and&format=builtin-long&config=htdig-wk (as of October 25, 2007).

[59] "Human Security and Livelihoods of Rural Afghans, 2002–2003" in United Nations Development Programme, 2004b.

national Crisis Group report, efforts to help are also often inefficient, with sewing centers, for example, costing some $3,000 per beneficiary. Women's shelters are also very costly and often become permanent accommodations for women with no other options; this limits their capacity to help the larger community, as they could do if the aid they receive was paired with follow-on resettlement aid, for example.[60] Some efforts, such as the World Food Programme's Women's Bakery Project in Kabul, which employs several hundred women, although helpful, are still challenged by gender biases and long-term economic stagnation.[61] It is also not clear how many of these projects respond to the fundamental obstacles hampering wage-earning by women—the lack of mobility, the absence of child care, and the need for middlemen.

Critics also argue that despite the lip service paid to the importance of improving the condition of women, some donors have avoided programs targeting women, fearing the controversy that might be associated with such programs. Other donors are accused of engaging in activities with an eye to gathering attention, but not to sustainability.[62] The flip side of this is that communities in Afghanistan are aware of donor desires to assist women, and some attempt to leverage this to garner aid for the community in ways that will not necessarily lead to empowerment of women. For example, NGOs and international organizations (IOs) have helped to create new community decisionmaking structures that incorporate more women or, alternatively, all-female structures. These coexist with the traditional all-male structures, but aid is funneled through the women's organizations. Certainly, this increases female participation, but there are some questions regarding whether this truly means greater female influence, or whether it just creates the gender equivalent of Potemkin villages, fictional female participation intended to please the international audience and attract aid. Skeptics note that the women in these "women's *shuras*" serve with the

---

[60] International Crisis Group, 2003.

[61] Womankind Worldwide, 2002, available at http://www.womankind.org.uk/cgi-bin/htsearch?words=Taking+Stock&method=and&format=builtin-long&config=htdig-wk (as of October 25, 2007).

[62] Ibid.

permission of the males of their households.[63] There is reason to think that communities go along with the programs to get the aid, perhaps "padding" structures with women to make sure they get the funds.[64] In some cases, communities may view aid going to women as second-best but are willing to accept it because it will increase household income broadly, creating new skills and leveraging old ones.[65] One could argue that over time, the simple fact of women participating in these new structures, however fictitious their actual authority is, will translate into influence. But there is the danger that these approaches put more pressure on female leaders to deliver good results, to the benefit of all, than they put on their male "counterparts," who continue to be the ones truly in charge.[66] Of even more concern is whether communities misrepresent intentions and efforts, for instance, in regard to plans to educate girls and boys equally, while they are actually allocating resources to benefit men more than women.[67]

As the World Bank rightly points out, programs to increase female involvement in Afghanistan's economy can have two possible goals. The first is to make women more productive in work they already do. This can have important results for Afghanistan as a whole and for all of its citizens, men and women, and is crucial to raising the living standards of some of Afghanistan's poorest families. The second possible goal is that of increasing the participation of women in the paid labor force. This is also important, and not only for equity reasons. The World Bank cites significant analysis and literature to argue that "gender-based restrictions on economic participation lower overall production and output per head" and reduce profits and growth. It notes that "a considerable share of the export success of the South East Asian economies was based on female-intensive light manufacturing."[68] This

---

[63] Wafa and Nader, 2005; Afghanistan Research and Evaluation Unit, 2005.

[64] Afghanistan Research and Evaluation Unit, 2005.

[65] Wakefield, 2005.

[66] Wakefield and Bauer, 2005.

[67] Ibid.

[68] World Bank, 2005.

echoes the argument made by Isobel Coleman that a high positive economic impact is yielded by educating women and ensuring their involvement in the economy, particularly in agriculture, where educating women may increase farm yields more than does increasing access to land or fertilizer for the population as a whole.[69]

In Chapter One, we discussed the role of women's equity in society in reducing interstate conflict. We find there are similar trends for conflict within a state, trends in which economic participation is a vital part. Employment can lessen the sense of fragmentation for women— or the rate at which people are marginalized and separated within a society—through the provision of job opportunities outside the home and a minimizing of household responsibilities, thereby heightening the availabilty of social connections and group bonds. Fragmentation, which is listed as one of the key pieces of structural violence that prompts intrastate conflict, can be considerably reduced through such interactions, prompting a greater sense of group and state security.[70]

Both goals are important, and both are critical to the development of Afghanistan and its economy. Assisting women to become more productive in the work that they already do increases their part in the overall labor force. Increasing the participation of women in the paid labor force, however, is far more difficult and requires programs not just to train more women in traditional tasks and ensure that they have access to loans, but also to find ways for them to get products to market on their own and to help them move into other parts of the economy.

Assuming that both goals are to be pursued, the programs and the measurement of their success must be reexamined. Some policy actions that have been recommended to boost women's participation in the labor force focus on increasing education more broadly. This is indeed crucial. Education and training, aside from providing skills, appear to increase women's roles in household and community decisionmaking. Women report that following training, men see them as having valuable knowledge to contribute, lowering the barriers to their

---

[69] Coleman, 2004a.

[70] Caprioli, 2005.

participation.[71] However, greater female participation should not be assumed to be self-perpetuating. Women in Afghanistan who are more mobile take advantage of opportunities to seek income but continue to confine other, younger women of their household to traditional tasks. Education of girls will remain controversial, as concern is voiced that educated women will leave the home and the community. Increased female participation in the economy may not help this matter in the near term. Female-headed households do not appear to be more likely to send their daughters to school than are male-headed households.[72] Thus, education of girls and women must include appropriate incentives to ensure that communities see advantages to it, which they presently may not. Finally, educating boys and men may also have important positive effects. Some evidence suggests that better-educated husbands correlate with more freedom for women to engage in public business.[73] That said, education is not the whole answer—in other states in the region, although education for women has improved, employment rates have lagged behind.[74]

In addition to education, literacy, and skills training, access to markets and mobility are critical. One recommendation is to have the women who do have access to bazaars, such as elderly childless widows, help bring the production of other women to market. Women-centered enterprises, such as women's orchards, are also suggested.[75] However, female-centered economic enterprises may be supported by communities in the short term, as long as they bring in aid, but may create a backlash in the longer term, with such efforts accused of dividing women and men within individual households and the community as a whole. Preventing such responses would require careful management of the situation in each community by donors and advisors—a diffi-

---

[71] Wafa and Nader, 2005; Afghanistan Research and Evaluation Unit, 2005.

[72] Wakefield, 2005; Schutte, 2006.

[73] World Bank, 2005.

[74] See World Bank Development Indicators, available at http://web.worldbank.org/ WBSITE/EXTERNAL/DATASTATISTICS/0,,contentMDK:20398986~pagePK:641331 50~piPK:64133175~theSitePK:239419,00.html (as of October 25, 2007).

[75] Wafa and Nader, 2005; Afghanistan Research and Evaluation Unit, 2005; Grace, 2004.

cult task. An alternative solution may be to focus less on side-by-side female and male decisionmaking structures and more on integrating women into previously all-male structures.[76] This, however, presents even greater challenges.

The other critical question in designing more-effective projects and putting them into action is that of how to measure effectiveness and success. A frequent criticism of aid efforts is that insufficient attention is paid to assessing effectiveness to better target programs and funding.[77] Of course, assessments require data, and some effort has been made to gather information on women's economic participation in more-recent years. However, this information is often incomplete and filled with questionable assumptions. For example, the UNDP was unable to calculate a gender-empowerment measure (to show the participation of women in public life) for Afghanistan due to insufficient information.[78] The Central Statistical Office (CSO) Statistical Yearbook for 2003 estimates that because 30 percent of the people employed in agriculture in Afghanistan are estimated to be women, and agricultural workers constitute 80 percent of the workforce, women make up 30 percent of the workforce. This rather questionable arithmetic is also repeated by the UNDP Human Development report.[79] With no data available on nonagricultural wage rates, the National Human Development Report followed the UNDP's lead and estimated women's wage rates to be 75 percent that of men's, a rather high number, corresponding to comparative wage rates in modern Western societies.[80]

There are two key issues to consider in collecting data on female economic participation. The first is that conventional calculations will fail to take women's contributions properly into account because so much of their contribution is not monetized. Moreover, women's work, monetized and otherwise, is consistently underreported in Afghani-

---

[76] Afghanistan Research and Evaluation Unit, 2005.

[77] Womankind Worldwide, 2002.

[78] United Nations Development Programme, 2004b.

[79] Womankind Worldwide, 2002.

[80] United Nations Development Programme, 2004b.

stan.[81] Thus, if the goal is to determine how women take part in the economy of the country, accounting methods that assess the extent of women's contributions on the basis of their labor rather than their pay will be more useful, if necessarily imprecise.[82] Moreover, as the World Bank points out, the chronic underestimation of women's inputs, monetized or otherwise, leads to overstatements of productivity of the economy as a whole, and certainly of men and various economic sectors. It also underestimates the labor requirements of tasks and production. This, of course, can lead to inefficient resource allocation by donors and governments.[83]

The second issue, however, is that the more traditional calculations, focusing on earned income, are also necessary, although data-gathering for them must be improved. Again, this returns to the question of improving the capacity for women to contribute economically in existing roles and to increase their scope for action. Calculations that focus on earned income are key indicators of success in the goal of increasing their part in the paid labor force, and they provide a sense of women's empowerment in that economy, their capacity for independent life and action, and the fullness of their participation as citizens and economic actors. In Afghanistan, as elsewhere, paid work is accorded a respect that unpaid work often is not, and to the extent that women are barred from paid work and/or discriminated in their performance of it, they remain second-class citizens.

Thus, improvement is needed in measuring both the work that women do and their part in the overall labor force. As the Afghanistan Research and Evaluation Unit recommends, gender-equity strategies and benchmarks within programs need to be improved, as must means of reviewing progress.[84] The core question is how to do that.

Estimates of nonmonetized contributions to the economy must be a core component of any studies of Afghanistan, if only because so

---

[81] World Bank, 2005.

[82] United Nations Development Programme, 2004c.

[83] World Bank, 2005.

[84] Wakefield and Bauer, 2005.

much of the economy is now informal. Much of this estimation will have to stem from field research and interviews, and it will continue to be difficult to acquire solid data in this area. Still, discussing the issues, presenting the anecdotal evidence, and identifying the data gaps can be helpful in their own right. To some extent, comparative figures from elsewhere in Afghanistan or from the work of other organizations can be used to assign monetary values to nonmonetized work.

In terms of measuring effects, output measures that assess not immediate impact (money provided), but second- and third-order effects (standards of living), can be useful in determining whether programs are effective. This is particularly true if the output measures are coupled with interview research that asks whether or not a certain program contributed to improved living standards. Programs that provide equipment should be monitored on a regular basis to see whether and how the equipment is being used, by whom it is being used, and whether it contributes to women's and households' livelihoods and standards of living.

These output measures are also important for ensuring that programs do not run counter to other goals. It is critical to determine that efforts to provide economic outlets for women do not undermine long-term efforts to educate girls, for example. Households will choose to have young children work rather than go to school if the child labor provides a needed economic input. Ensuring that this is not a choice that parents of girls face should be a goal of policy and programs. Programs should not contribute to child labor and continuing low literacy among girls. One way to assess success in this area is to follow individual cases. Another is to assess the correlations, if any, between programs and the enrollment, retention, and success of young girls in school.[85]

Similarly, it is important to follow programs over time to ensure that they continue to have desired effects. Efforts to give women more direct access to markets will probably require some trial and error to be effective. Various funders and implementers can learn from one

---

[85] For a discussion of how to measure the effectiveness of education of girls, see Unterhalter, Challender, and Rajagopalan (2005).

another by sharing information about their programs, and they should be encouraged to do so. Broad education programs should also be monitored through public-opinion polling and other assessment techniques to determine whether they are, indeed, affecting views of gender and women's issues.

Clarity about the goals of programs is also important. Implementers should be up front with themselves and donors about whether they are seeking to build on women's capacity to contribute in traditional ways, to expand female economic participation, or both. Clearer statements of goals will also support better development of metrics of success and effectiveness.

Dupree writes that while most women in rural areas are uneducated and untrained, the experience of the past decades has at least brought about an increased awareness of the benefits of health care and education. The war years also brought those women some increased power, while taking away a great deal of capacity. Most of the women in this group are likely to continue to participate in economic growth and reform through traditional means, but they may take advantage of new opportunities. Dupree also notes that Afghanistan has a small group of women with significant professional training and experience, as well as a commitment to at least a measure of equality. A somewhat larger group may see itself as less political, seeking simply the option of working and contributing to their country and their family.[86] These are the women who, alongside men in similar circumstances, can be the drivers of Afghanistan's economic reform—if they have the economic opportunities they need to succeed. Moreover, increasing the options available to all of Afghanistan's women will shrink the first group and grow the second, and, particularly, the third. Aside from developing a true constituency for change, this is necessary to enable today's Afghanistan to succeed at peace. But to move forward effectively, both programs and the capacity to assess them must improve. This will continue to be a challenging endeavor. It will take tremendous effort and significant time, for the problem is as much social and cultural as it is

---

[86] Dupree, 1998.

legal and structural. However, it is critical to Afghanistan's success that the effort be undertaken and given the priority that is appropriate to its goal: the full utilization of all of Afghanistan's human potential.

CHAPTER SIX

A Case Study: The National Solidarity Program

With its explicit gender-related goals and the visible presence of foreign implementers, Afghanistan's National Solidarity Program (NSP) could have been expected to invoke the sort of resistance to women's participation in nation-building that we discussed in Chapter One. A large number of NGOs were deployed to the field to implement and oversee the program, and their records provide rich material for understanding and assessing the processes on the ground. This case study illustrates that while it was not easy to obtain the participation of women, neither was this in any instance a "deal-breaker" or even a major source of discord. Rather, what was required was an ongoing interactive process in which obstacles and local concerns were continuously met with discourse and new solutions.

Overview of the Program

After the fall of the Taliban, the new government of Afghanistan, its people, and its supporters faced the challenge of rebuilding the nation based on democratic principles. Within this process, the NSP is a unique, large-scale development and reconstruction program that not only involves communities but is actually driven by them. It empowers communities to plan, manage, and monitor development projects of their own design. This approach ensures that the development projects are tailored to each community's particular needs; at the same time, it builds the capacity of the communities themselves to manage this process in the future. The structure of NSP fosters and develops skills and attitudes needed for local governance.

Under the auspices of NSP, communities establish a local governance structure (a Community Development Council, or CDC) that must be elected by the community and must incorporate previously marginalized groups, including women. The CDC is responsible for developing a community development plan, which is based on the identified and prioritized needs of the community, and for managing block grants to finance development and reconstruction projects. Throughout the process, CDCs work closely with facilitating partners (FPs) that assist with services such as training, technical assistance, and monitoring. There are currently 24 FPs, which were selected by the Afghan government.[1]

The Afghan Ministry for Rural Rehabilitation and Development (MRRD) launched the NSP in 2003 with financial support from several bilateral and multilateral donors: the World Bank, the European Union, and the governments of Canada, Denmark, Germany, Japan, Norway, the United Kingdom, and the United States.[2] The program has already expanded to operate in 34 provinces and 193 districts[3] and is intended to reach 20,000 rural communities by June 2007.[4] At the

---

[1] The FPs are the Agency for Technical Cooperation and Development (ACTED), Aga Khan Development Network (AKDN), Action Aid (AA), Afghan Development Agency (ADA), Afghan Aid (AAD), Bangladesh Rural Advancement Committee (BRAC), Cooperative for American Remittances to Europe (CARE), Coordination of Humanitarian Assistance (CHA), Concern, Danish Committee for Aid to Afghan Refugees (DACAAR), German Agro-Action (GAA), Ghazni Rural Support Program (GRSP), International Rescue Committee (IRC), Mission d'Aide au Développement des Economies Rurales (MADERA), Norwegian Project Office/Rural Rehabilitation Association for Afghanistan (NPO/RRA), Oxford Committee for Famine Relief (Oxfam), Ockenden International (OI), People in Need (PI), Relief International (RI), Swedish Committee for Afghanistan (SCA), Sanayee Development Foundation (SDF), Solidarites, Aide Humanitaire d'Urgence (Solidarités), United Nations Human Settlement Program (UN-HABITAT), and Zuid Oost Azie Refugee Care (ZOA).

[2] "Donors to the National Solidarity Program," NSP web site, http://www.nspafghanistan.org/the_donors/index_eng.html (as of October 25, 2007).

[3] National Solidarity Program, 2005c.

[4] National Solidarity Program, 2006, p. 2.

end of 2005, a total of $158 million had been disbursed to approximately 8,000 CDCs for more than 14,000 subprojects.[5]

Gender Mainstreaming

The inclusion of women and other marginalized groups has been a priority of the NSP since its inception in 2003. The policies and practices to facilitate this inclusion have developed as the program has grown. Throughout each implementation phase, the government of Afghanistan and the FPs have collected information about the opportunities, challenges, and successes of female inclusion. The MRRD analyzes this information and revises the program, its requirements, and its recommendations each year. As the NSP develops, its gender mainstreaming has evolved from simply including women on paper to working to ensure their active participation and empowerment. The current version of the NSP Operations Manual identifies gender equity as one of the four guiding principles for program implementation.[6] In 2005, the NSP developed a gender policy to determine practical measures to promote effective and equitable participation in the program. Table 6.1 lists policies and practices to promote gender equity throughout the program cycle.[7]

Lessons learned from the field—particularly those reported by the initial FPs—informed these policies and practices. The early experiences indicated that it is possible to achieve gender equity without compromising cultural and religious norms, provided the FPs devote adequate time to working with community leaders early in the community-mobilization process and throughout program implementation.[8] The need for community involvement in incorporating women is consistent with the fundamental principle of the NSP: The community must drive the development process.

---

[5] National Solidarity Program, 2005b.

[6] National Solidarity Program, 2006, p. 2.

[7] Ibid., p. 11.

[8] National Solidarity Program, 2006, p. 11.

Table 6.1
Policies and Practices to Promote Gender Equity Throughout the NSP Cycle

Principle	NSP Policies and Practices
Gender equity in NSP participation	• Gain early agreement with community leaders about the ways in which women can participate in CDCs in a culturally acceptable manner. • Organize parallel meetings for men and women so that women do not need to mix publicly with men. Even if mixed meetings are acceptable, it may be better for women to hold separate meetings so they can feel free to participate and speak openly. • Maintain records of participants in events and meetings, disaggregated by gender (particularly those related to community development planning).
Gender equity in CDC representation	• Organize separate voting venues for men and women to encourage more women to vote.
Gender equity in access to NSP information	• If there are cultural constraints to holding mixed-gender meetings, have the communities elect a male and a female representative from each cluster and organize male and female CDC subcommittees. Explain that male and female subcommittees have equal standing under the CDC. • Help communities identify methods for sharing information and coordinating just decisionmaking between the subcommittees. At a minimum: 1. Officers of each subcommittee should serve on the CDC Executive Coordination Committee, which finalizes and approves (signs) all NSP forms. 2. Minutes of all subcommittee/committee meetings should be shared between groups.
Gender equity in access to NSP training	• Ensure that program information such as the "public notice board" is posted in a public place that is easily accessible to men and women. If a mosque is chosen for posting information, another posting place accessible by women should also be chosen. • Ensure equitable delivery of training to male and female CDC members. At a minimum, all key officers (chairperson, treasurer, and secretary) of both subcommittees should be trained.
Gender equity in decisionmaking and control of project assets	• Inform community leaders that at least one NSP-funded subproject should be prioritized by women and managed by the women's CDC subcommittee. • Ensure that all NSP forms are signed by at least two male and two female officers.

SOURCE: National Solidarity Program, 2006.

Recognizing the importance of involving women in Afghanistan's nation-building, several FPs are focusing on gender mainstreaming within their own programming. For example, after the NSP's first year of implementation, the Agency for Technical Cooperation and Development (ACTED) felt that women's inclusion was "not real and meaningful." It addressed this by establishing a new department to address gender issues in detail.[9] An informal gender committee of the Danish Committee for Aid to Afghan Refugees (DACAAR) provided recommendations on gender issues, and the Afghan Development Agency (ADA) is in the process of developing a gender policy and strategy.[10] The Cooperative for American Remittances to Europe (CARE) has hired a full-time gender advisor.[11] The mainstreaming of gender through the broader NSP guidelines and specific actions by FPs can facilitate the inclusion of women in all levels of the NSP.

The Role of Women in the NSP

Despite continued challenges for the inclusion of women in the nation-building process, the NSP has made significant progress in this area. It is continually reviewing policies and practices that impact women's participation and making revisions to increase its effectiveness in including women. Within the NSP, women play three different roles: as implementers (working for the MRRD and FPs), as participants (voting for and serving as CDC representatives), and as beneficiaries (being the target population of community-development projects).

Women as NSP Implementers

Women participate as implementers at all levels of the NSP. Although the NSP Operations Manual does not have specific requirements for female staff, the evaluation criteria for FPs include inclusion of female employees—particularly at the field level. As stated in an evaluation by UN-HABITAT, the program's oversight consultant, "Where feasible, the Facilitating Partner is expected to recruit and deploy female field staff to enable involvement of women in the targeted commu-

---

[9] Brooke Stearns, ACTED survey response, received via email, February 7, 2006.

[10] Brooke Stearns, GRSP survey response, received via email, January 23, 2006.

[11] Brooke Stearns, CARE survey response, received via email, January 22, 2006.

nities in the prioritization, decision-making, and implementation of projects."[12]

Research by the Afghanistan Research and Evaluation Unit (AREU) highlights the importance of female field staff to facilitate female participation in the NSP. Male staff members may not be able to contact village women and may themselves have gender biases.[13] FPs acknowledge that such biases are present among some of their staff. Although there has been no systematic way to eliminate these gender biases, individual FPs are working to address the issue. Almost all of the FPs that participated in a recent email survey reported that their staffs receive gender-training programs that provide multiday workshops and pamphlets. In the NSP itself, male and female staff are expected to perform the same tasks. In 2004, the NSP held a monitoring and evaluation workshop in which 15 of the 45 participants were women. Although men and women sat separately and men dominated the discussion on the first day of the workshop, by the third day, facilitators instructed male and female staff to sit together and encouraged participation by all staff. One of the facilitators remarked, "While things may not change completely within three days, they surely learnt how women and men can work together."[14]

One of the FPs, ACTED, analyzed women's participation in the NSP and found it to be highly correlated with the active presence of female field staff. Several FPs reported that they practice positive discrimination to hire female staff members at all levels and particularly strive to have equal numbers of female and male field staff. However, recruitment of female staff is difficult because of education requirements and women's reluctance to work outside of the home, due to both local norms and family resistance.[15] Finding qualified female staff was the most commonly cited challenge FP survey respondents face in including women in the NSP in any role.

---

[12] United Nations Human Settlements Programme, 2004.

[13] Boesen, 2004, p. 17.

[14] Ministry of Rural Rehabilitation and Development, *MRRD Newsletter*, July 2004.

[15] Boesen, 2004, p. 18.

The difficulties of hiring (and retaining) female staff are also endemic to the type of work offered through the NSP. The work is particularly challenging for married female staff members, since it involves long hours and long commutes to work or extended stays in the area of operation. For example, German Agro-Action (GAA) female staff members remain in the field for three weeks each month because of the remoteness of their areas of operation. There are also some cultural constraints against having female staff operating in the field by themselves, so most of them are accompanied by a male relative, called a *maharam*.[16] GAA provides per diem and accommodations for *maharams*. ADA and Oxfam also reported that they will cover the costs of *maharams* whenever possible.[17] Female staff who must remain at the district office during the week or for even longer periods have the additional problem of needing to arrange for others to take care of their children.[18]

Although FPs have found ways of reducing the cultural barriers that may prohibit women from working as NSP field staff, many women still prefer not to commit to being away from home for long periods of time—particularly those who have families to care for. A report by UN-HABITAT states that "it is still difficult to find qualified and competent women who are prepared to go out into the communities to talk to the women in their homes."[19]

The challenge of employing women is further complicated by resistance from mullahs. ACTED explained that mullahs in some provinces were opposed to women working, especially for foreign NGOs. These mullahs provided misinformation about the FPs' female staff members in Friday noon prayers. They broke off relations with families of female staff and called on other villagers to do the same. ACTED found that poor and out-of-date knowledge of Islam, limited understanding of the NSP, and a sense of isolation due to no or limited roles for mullahs in

---

[16] Brooke Stearns, GAA survey response, received via email, January 23, 2006.

[17] Brooke Stearns, ADA survey response, received via email, January 29, 2006, and Oxfam survey response, received via email, January 31, 2006.

[18] Boesen, 2004, p. 18.

[19] United Nations Human Settlements Programme, 2004.

the NSP contributed to this resistance. Therefore, it created a pamphlet intended to legitimize women's presence in social affairs based on the Quran and international laws to convince the village mullahs to support female participation in the NSP.[20] The pamphlet, which includes Quranic verses and *hadiths*, was given to NSP community trainers to use in their communities.[21]

The general security situation in Afghanistan poses yet another challenge for employing women. Threats have been made against NGOs that employ female staff and against the females and their families. However, some FPs have found ways of working around this tenuous security environment—for example, when the security situation worsens, ADA female staff members work from home.[22] Nevertheless, the threat itself may be dissuading eligible women from working for NGOs.

Despite these challenges,

• Half of the Ockenden (a UK-registered charity) senior staff is female.
• Approximately one-third of the Swedish Committee for Afghanistan (SCA), the Sanayee Development Foundation (SDF), and Solidarité Afghanistan Belgium (SAB) district and field staff are women.[23]
• Approximately one-fifth of Ockenden's district and field staff are women.[24]
• More than one-quarter of Oxfam's field office staff are women, and almost half of the community social organizers are women.[25]

---

[20] "Gender pamphlet presentation to FP Meeting," ACTED NSP/Gender Department.

[21] ACTED survey response, received via email, February 7, 2006.

[22] ADA survey response, received via email, January 29, 2006.

[23] SCA survey response, received via email, January 28, 2006; SDF survey response, received via email, January 31, 2006; and Solidarité survey response, received via email, February 15, 2006.

[24] Ockenden survey response, January 28, 2006; SDF survey response, January 31, 2006; and Solidarité survey response, May 14, 2006.

[25] Oxfam survey response, received via email, January 31, 2006.

- One-third of Afghan Aid's social organizers are women.[26]
- Thirty percent of Concern's district and field staff are women.[27]
- Twenty-seven percent of GAA's district staff are women.[28]
- Twenty-two percent of the Ghazni Rural Support Program (GRSP) field staff are women.[29]
- Sixteen percent of the Coordination of Humanitarian Assistance (CHA) field staff are women.[30]

The backgrounds of female staff members vary by their positions and the geographic location of the program. District-level staff tend to have secondary and sometimes tertiary education and to be from the district's capital or another city. The female field staff are literate and tend to have some secondary education. To the extent possible, they are from the rural areas where the program is operating, but often FPs rely on females who live near the district office.

Women as Participants

Female community members can play key roles as participants in the NSP program in various aspects of implementation: community mobilization and awareness, CDC elections, and CDC participation.

Community Mobilization and Awareness. Access to information about the NSP is crucial for participation in the program, particularly while the program is striving to establish its reputation. AREU research found that more men than women were informed about and understood the NSP.[31] Women were less able to attend NSP information session due to *purdah* (gender-based) restrictions.[32] This is particularly

---

[26] AAD survey response, February 11, 2006.

[27] Concern survey response, received via email, January 31, 2006.

[28] GAA survey response, received via email, January 23, 2006.

[29] GRSP survey response, received via email, January 28, 2006.

[30] CHA survey response, received via email, January 28, 2006.

[31] Boesen, 2004, p. 24.

[32] Ibid, p. 23.

true among older and illiterate women.[33] While a lack of understanding of the NSP may explain some difficulties for female participation, more deep-seated beliefs about gender roles may also be an obstacle. AREU research included comments by female villagers describing the NSP as "men's business" and stating that they are too busy to remember the information about it.[34] ACTED commented, "You will see women who themselves say that they can not understand anything and they are brought to this world just do to these [household tasks such as baby-sitting, cooking, animal husbandry, and farm work] activities."[35] CARE and ACTED found that many women lack interest in the proposal or refuse to participate.[36] But as more communities successfully incorporate women in the NSP programming, there is some "spillover" effect that increases female participation in neighboring communities.

Nearly all of the FPs that responded to the email survey stated that they faced resistance to female participation in the early stages of program implementation. AAD indicated that they had success in involving women in many communities where they had been working for several years and had established trust—prior to the NSP, ADA organized women's resource centers.[37] DACAAR identified resistance at the provincial, district, and village levels to the involvement of women in the NSP.[38] However, several FPs reported that the resistance diminished as the communities became more familiar with the FP and the NSP. Several FPs reported that they had held numerous meetings to discuss the NSP with community members.

One community so strongly opposed female participation that it declined to participate in the NSP entirely. Members of the community also said they would attack CARE female staff if they entered the community, threatened CARE's community developer, and tried to

---

[33] Ibid, p. 24.

[34] Ibid.

[35] ACTED survey response, received via email, February 7, 2006.

[36] Boesen, 2004, p. 50,

[37] ADA survey response, received via email, January 29, 2006.

[38] GRSP survey response, received via email, January 23, 2006.

present written refusal to participate. The community developer convinced them to withdraw their written refusal, and CARE staff held regular meetings to discuss the community's concerns. After approximately seven months, the community agreed to implement the NSP. Female voter turnout was more than 70 percent.[39]

One particularly useful strategy for overcoming culturally based resistance to female participation in the NSP is to explain women's rights and participation from an Islamic point of view. ACTED, CHA, DACAAR, GRSP, and SDF all reportedly garner support for female participation through this approach.[40] GRSP and IRC indicated that they also work with mullahs to generate support for female participation in the NSP.[41] In Afghanistan, religion and cultural norms have become deeply intertwined as a result of the Taliban rule and low levels of literacy, so the Islamic principles and the cultural norms and customs are unclear. For example, Islam views obtaining education as obligatory for both men and women; however, many girls do not attend school because of cultural norms. Many Islamic principles and verses from the Quran can be utilized to garner community support for female involvement in the NSP and nation-building efforts more broadly. The ACTED pamphlet uses Quranic verses or *hadiths* to indicate the importance and rights of female members of society and the importance of their participation in community development and in rebuilding the nation.[42]

Community Development Council Elections. The CDC is the decisionmaking body that oversees the implementation of NSP activities within the community. The use of CDCs was motivated, at least in part, by a desire to create a governance structure that represents previ-

---

[39] CARE survey response, received via email, January 22, 2006.

[40] Gender pamphlet presentation to FP Meeting, ACTED NSP/Gender Department; CHA Survey Response, January 28, 2006; GRSP survey response, January 23, 2006; GRSP survey response, January 28, 2006; SDF survey response, January 31, 2006.

[41] GRSP survey response, January 28, 2006; and Kakar, 2005, p. 26.

[42] Gender pamphlet presentation to FP meeting, ACTED NSP/Gender Department; CHA survey response, January 28, 2006; GRSP survey response, January 23, 2006; GRSP survey response, January 28, 2006; SDF survey response, January 31, 2006.

ously marginalized members of society, including women and return-
ees. Again, the inclusion of marginalized groups has evolved with the
program itself. In the first two years, only 40 percent of eligible voters
needed to vote in order for a CDC election to be valid.[43] This requirement enabled the election of CDCs without female voters. A 2004
AREU study found that this was the result of a conscious decision
by the NSP to enable valid elections even in conservative communities that might not allow women to vote. According to AREU, "the
political costs of excluding 'conservative' communities, which would
not allow women to participate in the elections, is considered more
critical than the potential exclusion of women that this rule provides
for, since mandatory registration and participation of women in the
electoral process could provide ammunition for radical Islamic opposition to the central government."[44] As the NSP became more grounded,
the Afghan government amended this policy. The recently revised NSP
Operations Manual stipulates that at least 60 percent of eligible voters
must vote for the election to be valid.[45]

The initial gender-inclusion strategy focused on efforts by FPs to
work within local communities to maximize female participation. IRC
and DACAAR were able to convince communities to allow women
to vote, provided the elections were segregated, with men voting for
male representatives and women voting for female representatives.[46]
The International Rescue committee (IRC) uses trained mullahs who
work with community religious leaders to allow female voting. This
approach identifies Islamic principles of women's rights (such as the
right to take part in consultations through elections and councils)
and venues (such as Friday sermons) to garner community support for
female participation.[47]

AREU found that "the NSP views the participation of women as
a process, rather than something that can be decreed, and expects that

---

[43] National Solidarity Program, 2004, p. 16.

[44] Boesen, 2004, p. 8.

[45] National Solidarity Program, 2006, p. 14.

[46] Kakar, 2005, p. 25.

[47] Kakar, 2005, p. 26.

this will gradually take root through a culturally sensitive facilitation effort, and through the example of benefits achieved where women are enabled to participate in the elections as beneficiaries of specific subprojects that address their needs."[48] Consistent with this assessment, GAA reported that the challenges for female participation have decreased over time as the NSP has become better known.[49]

AREU identified the initial voting policy that did not require female participation as potentially problematic in that it reinforced existing gender relations and power structures in decisionmaking. Requiring female participation could present a venue for altering gender and power dynamics within communities.[50] The 2003 CDC elections were close to reaching the target of 40 percent of voters being women. In addition, a larger percentage of registered women voted than men: 75 percent of the women and 68 percent of the men.[51] AREU found that in 11 districts, 43 percent of the registered voters were women, 86 percent of the female registered voters did vote, and 44 percent of those who voted in the election were women.[52]

To facilitate female participation in voting, the NSP Operations Manual allows for separate female voting stations and individually designed methods for casting votes for female candidates when their names cannot be listed on ballots.[53] In practice, women's elections have tended to take place in private houses (whereas men's elections are generally in public spaces), and many of them have used "open voting," i.e., voting by a show of hands rather than secret ballots. Women in the communities of one district indicated that the open-voting process was more free and fair than secret voting.[54]

---

[48] Grenblatt-Harrison, O'Connell, and Gyan-Bryant, 2005..

[49] GAA survey response, received via email, January 23, 2006.

[50] Boesen, 2004, p. 8.

[51] Grenblatt-Harrison, O'Connell, and Gyan-Bryant, 2005.

[52] Boesen, 2004, pp. 33, 34.

[53] National Solidarity Program, 2006, p. 15.

[54] Boesen, 2004, p. 32.

Although the changes in the NSP policies require female participation in elections, they do not ensure that women's voices are heard in
them. AREU found that most women were told how to vote by male
relatives.[55] This is a cultural aspect that cannot be altered by mandate
or policy, but rather will, it is to be hoped, evolve as the program continues and fosters a culture of greater gender balance.

Community Development Council Participation. Since the inception of the NSP, many women have been elected to CDCs. In the first
352 villages that held NSP-supported elections (across five provinces),
2,289 women and 3,755 men were elected to CDCs.[56] Several FPs
reported that with time, women have been elected to CDCs even in the
more conservative areas. The 2006 revised NSP Operations Manual
specifies that each cluster of voters will elect two representatives for the
CDC: one male and one female. Each voter will cast one vote, and the
male and female who receive the most votes will be confirmed as CDC
representatives.[57]

Initial female participation was higher than expected, and mechanisms have been put into place to ensure continued female representation; however, empirical research has shown mixed results in terms of
active participation by women. CHA and SDF reported that women
CDC members do propose issues for consideration in the mixed
CDCs.[58] Ockenden reported that approximately 7 percent of mixed
CDC members are women, and they all attend and actively participate
in CDC meetings.[59]

Oxfam, however, found that attendance of women in mixed
CDCs was merely symbolic and that the women do not voice their
opinions.[60] ACTED reported that "in mixed CDCs the participation

---

[55] Ibid., p. 38.

[56] Coleman, 2004a.

[57] National Solidarity Program, 2006, pp. 14–16.

[58] CHA survey response, received via email January 28, 2006; SDF survey response, received
via email, January 31, 2006.

[59] Ockenden survey response, received via email, February 1, 2006.

[60] Oxfam survey response, received via email, January 31, 2006.

and attendance of women in [the] decision-making process is really low and very difficult."[61] Solidarités found that although women were elected to CDCs, they do not participate.[62] In 30 communities studied by AREU, only three women participated as full members of a mixed male-female CDC.[63] AREU found that although women were elected to mixed CDCs, their participation was problematic in all districts in its study. In one village, female elected representatives were prohibited by their husbands from participating in the CDCs.[64] Although there may be examples of successful active participation of women in mixed CDCs, this is clearly not the case in all situations.

One means of working around this challenge is to create female-only CDCs—in several communities, such CDCs were elected or informally established. In the case of the latter, interested women who had some degree of education and/or mobility in the community formed an informal female "CDC" through either recruitment by the FP staff or appointment by the community women.[65] Members of the women's CDCs (formal and informal) visit female community members to discuss household and community problems and ideas for women's projects.[66]

The informal CDCs generally serve in an advisory or lobbying role for specific projects the women deem important. The formally elected female CDCs theoretically would communicate with the male CDCs by sharing minutes or having a male relative serve as a messenger and represent the women in the male CDC.[67] AREU found, however, that communications between the women's meeting and the male-dominated CDC were often uncoordinated, if they existed at all.[68]

---

[61] ACTED survey response, received via email, February 7, 2006.

[62] Solidarités survey response, received via email, February 15, 2006.

[63] Wakefield and Bauer, 2005.

[64] Boesen, 2004, p. 38.

[65] Kakar, 2005, p. 25.

[66] Boesen, 2004, p. 54.

[67] Kakar, 2005, p. 25.

[68] Wakefield and Bauer, 2005.

The challenges of female participation in mixed CDCs and female-only CDCs underline the difficulties of truly mainstreaming gender in practice, rather than simply on paper.

AREU researchers assert that "the physical presence of women in local-level institutions is a false measure of achievement of gender goals."[69] Even where women are technically CDC participants, they are often still marginalized. And in communities where formal female CDCs exist, the male CDCs have the power to make the final decisions on community development projects, since they sign for the money, and the bank accounts are registered to them.[70] Several FPs have identified ways to empower the female CDCs, however. For example, DACAAR requires that subproject funding alternate between the male and female CDCs and has created separate accounts for the female CDCs; SCA requires that female CDC members sign and approve all projects, along with male members.[71] But despite these efforts, members of female-only CDCs indicated that their priorities overall are not adequately considered by the male CDC members.[72]

As a result, the 2005 national gender policy discontinued the NSP's system that permitted separate female and male CDCs. To facilitate the inclusion of women, FPs now have two options: (1) they can form gender-integrated CDCs with a single group of four officers, or (2) they can create separate male-only and female-only subcommittees with a single executive coordination committee consisting of two officers from each CDC.[73] This is a strategy that some FPs had already developed. For example, Solidarités' strategy for increasing female participation was to require that two of the executive committee members be women.[74]

---

[69] Ibid.

[70] Kakar, 2005, p. 25.

[71] Ibid.

[72] National Solidarity Program, 2005a.

[73] Coleman, 2004a.

[74] Solidarités survey response, recieved via email, February 15, 2006.

Some FPs have already experienced success in having women serve in leadership roles. ACTED found that as the NSP becomes more well-known, women are being elected to CDC leadership positions.[75] Each of the two provinces where GAA works has a CDC with a female chairperson, and there is a female CDC chairperson in one of the communities where GRSP is working.[76] In one of the communities where CARE is working, a woman was chosen as a candidate for CDC chairperson; however, she declined the nomination because of the required travel.[77]

If separate subcommittees are established, communities need to identify and implement methods to facilitate communication between them. One option is to have the subcommittees meet simultaneously, separated by a curtain, with messengers carrying communication between them. Alternatively, the subcommittees can meet separately, and representatives can attend each other's meeting, or representatives from both CDCs can hold their own meeting.[78] In some areas, female FP staff serve as liaison between the CDCs.[79]

One of the primary activities of the CDCs is to create a community development plan (CDP) that identifies priorities and subprojects. The NSP requires that a women's meeting be held to facilitate free and open discussion of community development priorities, and that at least one priority subproject identified by women be included in the CDP and designated for NSP funding.[80]

CHA described the process of creating a CDP that addressed gender issues in one community. The male CDC members proposed construction of a bath as their first priority. The female CDC members interjected to ask whether women would be allowed to use it. When the

---

[75] ACTED survey response, received via email, February 7, 2006.

[76] GAA survey response, received via email, January 23, 2006; and GRSP survey response, received via email, January 28, 2006.

[77] CARE survey response, received via email, January 22, 2006.

[78] Coleman, 2004a.

[79] Boesen, 2004, p. 56.

[80] National Solidarity Program, 2006, p. 16.

men responded that the women would not be allowed to, the women convinced the men to propose a school as the first priority, so that the project would address the needs of both male and female community members.[81] In addition, in one village where GRSP is working, female CDC members refuse to sign men's project proposals unless the men agree to a women's project.[82]

Although the policies of some CDCs address some of the challenges of female representation, they do not address other barriers. For example, another major impediment to female participation is the short time frame within which communities must establish CDCs. The current version of the NSP Operations Manual indicates that CDC elections should take place after the first month of program inception.[83] FPs report that this time frame does not allow communities to develop an understanding of the importance of female participation.[84] In addition, many FPs attribute the lack of female participation in CDCs to a "lack of confidence in their [women's] own skills due to lack of relevant management and leadership experience."[85] One of the FPs has developed a five-year strategy to cultivate female leaders. It has established women's groups who receive the same training as the CDC members (in management, proposal writing, accounting, and procurement) and who lobby for and implement small projects. This program is designed to prepare women to be active CDC members before the next CDC elections.[86]

Women as Beneficiaries

The fourth role women play is that of beneficiaries of community development projects undertaken under the auspices of the NSP. Two types of subprojects may be financed: public infrastructure and human-

---

[81] CHA survey response, received via email, 28 January 2006.

[82] GRSP survey response, received via email, 28 January 2006.

[83] National Solidarity Program, 2006, p. 24.

[84] Kakar, 2005, p. 28.

[85] Ibid.

[86] Ibid.

capital development. The former includes projects designed to (re)build or improve water and sanitation, irrigation, transportation, power, and public buildings such as schools, hospitals, and clinics. The latter are programs to develop knowledge and skills among community members to improve their standard of living. Within human-capital development, the NSP specifies two subcategories: general education (such as literacy and general health education) and productive-skills training (for income-generation projects such as kitchen gardens and animal husbandry). The NSP Operations Manual specifies that at least half of the individuals participating in training programs must be women.[87] FPs can also utilize these subprojects to facilitate increased female participation in the NSP and empowerment more broadly—for example, ACTED encourages women CDC members to select literacy courses for projects, as this will address one of the root causes of limited female participation in CDCs.[88]

The 2004 NSP Operations Manual specified that a minimum of 10 percent of community block grants must be invested in projects directly benefiting women,[89] which tend to be related to education and health.[90] One of the first community projects to be implemented under the NSP was the creation of a girls' school; the project was proposed by the female CDC and approved by a majority of votes.[91] The women were also interested in income-generation projects, which can account for a maximum of 10 percent of the total block grant.[92] CHA reported that most of the income-generation projects women propose are approved.[93] Although GAA found that projects that focus on women and have a real impact on their situation are primarily income-generation projects, this type of project raises some questions: Do the products meet the

---

[87] National Solidarity Program, 2006, p. 3.

[88] ACTED survey response, received via email, February 7, 2006.

[89] National Solidarity Program, 2004.

[90] Boesen, 2004, p. 54.

[91] United Nations Office for the Coordination of Human Affairs, 2004.

[92] National Solidarity Program, 2004.

[93] CHA survey response, received via email, January 28, 2006.

quality standards of the market? Is there access to markets? How are the proceeds used?[94]

Despite the NSP policies, men's projects are often prioritized above women's projects. AREU found that when funding was limited, women's projects would not be included in the priority subprojects, but would be relegated to the waiting list.[95] GAA indicated that female CDC members may not prioritize women's projects because they want the projects to benefit the entire community.[96] Oxfam indicated that, typically, the first community project is selected by men, and the second is selected by women.[97] But despite these prioritization issues, several FPs indicated that projects proposed by female CDCs or CDC members are approved and implemented:

- Nearly half of the approved community projects in the CDCs that Ockenden is working with were proposed by women.[98]
- Of the 27 community development projects proposed by women in the areas where CHA is working, 21 are being implemented.[99]
- Nineteen percent of the community development projects implemented in areas where SDF is the FP and 12 percent in the communities where Oxfam works specifically target women and were proposed by female CDCs.[100]

Conclusion

Since its inception, the NSP has prioritized the inclusion of women at all levels of its implementation. It has overcome significant challenges

---

[94] GAA survey response, received via email, January 23, 2006.

[95] Boesen, 2004, p. 54.

[96] GAA survey response, received via email, January 23, 2006.

[97] Oxfam survey response, received via email, January 31, 2006.

[98] Ockenden survey response, received via email, 28 January 2006.

[99] CHA survey response, received via email, January 28, 2006.

[100] SDF survey response, received via email, January 31, 2006; Oxfam survey response, received via email January 31, 2006.

to increasingly involving women in nation-building. We present three key findings from the NSP's experiences to date.

First, *gender mainstreaming is a process rather than a policy.* Female participation in nation-building has developed and will continue to evolve as the program and the FPs establish relationships and reputations within the local communities. For example, although the NSP was initially structured so that female voting was not required in CDC elections, within two years this policy was revised. Working slowly, establishing local support, and developing gender mainstreaming, rather than imposing dramatic changes, appear to be successfully and increasingly involving women in Afghanistan's nation-building process.

Second, *fostering local support is essential for involving women in nation-building.* As FPs develop relationships within communities and garner support from local leaders, the inclusion of women in the NSP becomes more feasible. Community-driven development is the cornerstone of the NSP, and this same grassroots support is needed for gender mainstreaming.

Third, *the FPs have utilized local culture, including Islamic principles, to promote female participation in the NSP.* FPs are working with local mullahs and using Islamic principles and passages to garner support. This practice requires not only cultural appreciation, but also cultural understanding. Although many nation-building programs strive to be culturally sensitive, the NSP FPs use local culture to support the program.

The 2005 gender policy resulted in substantial changes in the NSP Operations Manual intended to further foster active female participation in all levels of the NSP. Most notably, separate women's CDCs will be discontinued, CDCs will consist of an equal number of male and female representatives, and leadership roles will be divided between men and women. The impacts of these changes on the participation of women in the program should be examined to gain a further understanding of the NSP's progress in facilitating women's participation in nation-building.

CHAPTER SEVEN

Recommendations

Introduction

In the coming years, nation-building missions in complex post-conflict environments will continue to engage the United States and the international community. Policymakers and practitioners alike must take care to evaluate present nation-building exercises. Clearly, this evaluation will need to be outcomes-based and will need to focus on the female majority of the populations in question.

Recommendation 1: Have a Goal-Oriented Focus

Intervention goals should be clear and unequivocal. Stakeholders in post-conflict contexts would most likely agree that promoting women's rights is a general goal, but at times, agreeing to a common definition of women's rights is a challenge. Women's rights can mean different things to different parties, and the issue is continually muddled by cross-cultural understandings of the term. Our purpose here is not to advocate for one particular definition, but rather to encourage those involved in nation-building to focus on creating a clear institutional understanding of their goals with regard to women that is transparent to outside parties and national actors alike.

Groups with a stake in post-conflict Afghanistan may define women's rights in many different ways. The term could mean promoting respect for the traditional activities of women; conversely, it could mean promoting their access to nontraditional roles. The definition provides a frame for creating goals, which in turn motivates programming and execution, which can be advanced via different structures. It is possible that the goal of achieving "women's rights" without proper clarification could lead to incompatible programs and mixed outcomes. In addition to clarifying their understanding of women's rights, implementers should also be up front with themselves and with donors about whether they are seeking to build on women's capacity to contribute in traditional ways, to expand female participation, or both. If they are seeking both, they might be intending a parallel approach, depending on their assessment of what is desirable and achievable for particular subgroups within the population, or they might have a sequenced approach in mind, with a bolstering of women's traditional role seen as a midway point toward the ultimate goal of a more modern vision of gender equality. Clearer statements of goals will also support better development of metrics of success and effectiveness.

The goal for women's rights activities in Afghanistan should include both increasing access to nontraditional roles and strengthening women's capacity to earn a livelihood through the monetization of more-traditional activities. This goal presents several complications. It can be difficult for an organization to promote access to new roles and support for traditional roles at the same time. This could potentially create mixed messages as well as mixed outcomes for the organization's programs. The complications do not go away if multiple organizations focus on one goal or the other. Rather, taking this fairly aggressive social-engineering approach will require strong coordination among international and local NGOs and the Afghan government to suppress likely opposition to goals and programs and to successfully formulate a complex message for the population.

Recommendation 2: Build Up Reliance on Civil Society

Our second recommendation calls for continual development of the second-track and civil society, including developing indigenous programs for capacity-building. This will require long-term application of resources and structural support for indigenous community-level programs that encourage local leaders to accept both traditional and nontraditional roles for women. As is evident from our NSP case study, this process can boost effectiveness by drawing heavily on local culture. For Afghanistan, this means effective integration of Islamic principles and reliance on traditional forms of affiliation when promoting female participation. Awareness of local cultural needs allows indigenous programs to promote a more inclusive form of resource integration and creates community-level buy-in of overall goals, while the need for broader knowledge of what has worked in comparable situations, how the international community functions, and what resources are available make external participation essential as well.

Afghan women and their nascent humanitarian organizations must continue to play a critical role in service delivery and governance. They have already provided assistance in education, health care, supplying clean water, and political schooling. These governance and reconstruction efforts are especially critical in the southern and eastern parts of Afghanistan, where the Taliban and other insurgent groups have been most active. The humanitarian organizations give women an important opportunity to curb the power of insurgents and to support the Afghan government. International groups should continue to focus on building this indigenous infrastructure across several domains. Backlash against the continual empowerment of women is inevitable, but possible countermeasures include a formal institutionalization of mechanisms to support civil-social groups.

Civil-society mechanisms should strive for a comprehensive overhaul of the justice system in Afghanistan. International and local groups should work together to create comprehensive training programs for personnel in the judiciary and police forces, raising sensitivity for basic human rights. Civil-society groups should act to modify or abolish laws such as the 1970s-era penal code and regulations, customs, and practices that constitute discrimination against women in family matters. In particular, reform of the criminal-justice system should ensure that women are given legal equality with men in the right to freely choose a spouse, the right to enter into marriage only with full and free consent, and equal rights and responsibilities during marriage and its dissolution. Furthermore, Afghan authorities need to ensure that the law is implemented by the courts in a way that provides equality in practice between men and women. Social-service provision to ameliorate the effects of incomplete application of the laws and to assist the victims of abuses is an important part of this.

In economic matters, nation-builders should place high value not only on programs that make women more productive in the work they already do, but also on opening more opportunities for women. This means not simply training in traditional economic activities, but also ensuring access to loans, finding ways to help women get products to market on their own, and otherwise helping them to move into other parts of the economy. In the early phases of nation-building, it is common to designate mass employment opportunities for men. Road-building, for example, offers quick employment to large numbers of individuals. Thought needs to be given to equivalent culturally acceptable mass employment opportunities for women. In the first years of Afghan reconstruction, sewing projects were the only projects that occurred to external actors.

Such efforts challenge social mores and will be opposed by many men—and women—who view women's rights as a political, and not an economic, issue. However, traditional attitudes can also be tapped in support of these goals. For example, in Kabul, the establishment of a women's market, accessible only to female shoppers and with shops operated by women, aroused no objection and permitted women to break into the hitherto exclusive male domain of shopkeeping.

Again, these mechanisms need to be considered and implemented thoughtfully, in reference to a larger plan and with careful consideration of unintended consequences.

Overall, the nation-building community should seek to integrate both genders into businesses where possible. While creating female-centered economic enterprises may be supported by communities in the short term as long as they bring in aid, it could also create detrimental effects in the longer term, perpetuating a divide between women and men in the workplace. Studies of the far more advanced economies of the Gulf countries, in which parallel economic enterprises often exist, can shed greater light on the positive and negative aspects of this solution.[1] We believe that side-by-side female and male decisionmaking structures at all levels of society should be abolished in favor of integrating women into previously all-male structures and that the prior solution should at best be a transitional one.

Recommendation 3: Improve Data Collection

The United States and other international actors must work to improve their assessment strategies for measuring women's participation in Afghan life and in post-conflict situations in general. Data on the social well-being of women in the world are collected by several leading international organizations, including United Nations agencies and the World Bank. Unfortunately these data are hard to collect in conflict zones, making it difficult to establish baseline assessments for policy development and subsequent analysis of progress in reconstruction efforts. In Afghanistan, it is nearly impossible for organizations to collect data on simple, internationally recognized measures, let alone data on the sophisticated social indexes developed by UNESCO, UNDP, Oxfam, and UNICEF. However, intervention forces need data to gauge their effectiveness, just as local and international NGOs need the protection of intervention forces to collect the data. Only through such "analysis and coordination will policy makers overcome the obstacles that have historically impeded engagement,"[2] a lesson that is particularly salient in Afghanistan, where created systems of power are often out of touch with people on the ground. Collaboration on data collection, therefore, should be attainable, as it is in everyone's interest.

---

[1] In Saudi Arabia, Qatar, and other Muslim countries in the region, customs of strict gender segregation have opened professional opportunities for women—for example, in banking, where separate branches of banks cater to female clients and are staffed by women. To our knowledge, the economic consequences of duplicate institutions of this kind have not been systematically examined.

[2] Carment et al., 2006. For more on the data, see the Country Indicators for Foreign Policy Project, Carleton University, at http://www.carleton.ca/cifp/about.htm (as of October 25, 2007).

In states undergoing post-conflict reconstruction, data on indicators should be collected in three phases: First, reconstruction efforts should focus on opening basic public services and measuring access with regard to all the critical criteria in play (rural/urban, ethnicity, gender, etc.). The next effort, closely following the first, should focus on bringing in and supporting existing international data-collection organizations such as UNESCO, UNDP, and the World Bank, among others, so that data collection on areas of social well-being, using the Millennium Development Goals (a framework for measuring factors of development proposed by the United Nations) as a baseline, can begin. Using one or two indicators for each area would make it easier to focus limited resources and staff. Resources should be allocated early to help ministries organize and train for data collection. Finally, the international reconstruction team should work with the national government, international organizations, and local and international NGOs to develop a data-collection approach to measure outcomes in all sectors. This could include training and support for more-advanced data-collection techniques, such as developing and improving the national Education Management Information System (EMIS), which is used by most national education ministries and which passes education data on to UNESCO for the compilation of international datasets.[3]

One important contribution the Millennium Development Goals could make would be the establishment of a standard set of measures that could be used to measure progress in all post-conflict reconstruction efforts, not just in Afghanistan. Another benefit could be to create incentives for cross-coordination of planning and resources among international organizations toward the same goals. International groups could also assist by standardizing the known resources available for women in post-conflict situations, especially in local contexts. A collective and inclusive database could be used to categorize relevant information, such as international emergency-personnel locations and vital-resource locations. This information could be quickly accessed during an emergency situation, linking local groups via international oversight.

---

[3] Unterhalter, Challender, and Rajagopalan, 2005.

In economic terms, establishing meaningful data-collection mechanisms for Afghanistan will take a certain amount of creativity, as traditional calculations have continually failed to take into account the critical contribution women make to the Afghan economy. Much of women's economic contribution is not monetized, and the work of women is greatly underreported. To some extent, comparative figures from elsewhere could be used to provide monetary values to nonmonetized work in Afghanistan. Nation-building experts must seek out an alternative data-gathering methodology for the more-conventional pay-based calculations, to permit an assessment of how women's economic roles are changing, especially when paired with labor-based estimates. This process should include output measures that assess not only immediate impact (money provided), but also second- and third-order effects (standards of living), which can be useful in determining whether programs are effective. This is particularly true if the measures are coupled with interview research that asks whether or not programs contributed to improved living standards. Additionally, programs that provide equipment should be monitored on a regular basis to see whether and how the equipment is being used, by whom, and whether it contributes to women's and households' livelihoods and standard of living.

Data collection is also necessary from a security standpoint. Especially pressing are data measuring violence against women, which must include violence in the family. This information should be collected, institutionalized, and made publicly available. It should cover such issues as the causes of violence against women, including social attitudes, customs, and practices. It should look into the effects of such violence, the effectiveness of measures to counter it, and the social attitudes underlying it. This research could be done by an international organization such as the United Nations or by one of several NGOs in Afghanistan.

Recommendation 4: Resolve Contradictions

The process of nation-building is bound to create contradictions between preexisting and newly created social systems. Even in highly developed societies, new social systems can create volatile situations. Social change has an impact on highly emotive, power-based relations between state actors and requires continual reassessment of the values of all parties. Thus it is vital that resources be delegated to both predicting and resolving inherent social contradictions.

An excellent example of the contradictions created by social change is the disconnect that occurred in Afghanistan between Islamic law and the promotion of international human rights. Afghanistan's constitution promoted deference to the Quran on all issues while also pronouncing respect for international human rights and international conventions. The actual rules regarding the relationships between women and men remained unclear, and a host of regional and tribal traditions continue to hold sway, often in flagrant contradiction of both of the codes enshrined in the constitution: Islamic precepts *and* human rights. An overhaul of existing laws could create the legal framework necessary to overcome this contradiction, while a public education campaign could inform the Afghan people about the true precepts of Islam and the values of human rights, as well as the societal benefits of respecting them. The contradiction between the principles as they are written (in the constitution and in existing legal code) and as they are practiced is vast. Reformers must address that contradiction and create long-term plans to engage the Afghan population regarding women's rights as citizens. Indigenous NGOs must also work to keep the international community engaged. The ability to connect with resource networks will be essential.

These recommendations have a common emphasis on creating and sustaining local support. Push-down of reforms initiated from above and/or from outside has historically been the weak point in repeated efforts to modernize Afghanistan. Fostering local, community-based support for women's programs and extending that support into the provinces and to the lower strata of society are essential. As foreign actors develop relationships within communities and garner support from local leaders, the inclusion of women in policy programming will become more feasible. Multilayered development that obtains traction at the community level is the cornerstone of successful programs, and grassroots support is needed.

Promoting clarity in missions, supporting more-precise data-collection mechanisms that reflect how societies actually function and the role women play in them, and assistance in the promotion of civil society, all applied and implemented through a cultural framework, can create lasting success for both nation-builders and the women of Afghanistan.

Education and Health Indicators for Women and Girls

Education Indicators

The three main sources of national-level data on education of women and girls (as well as of men and boys) are the following organizations:

- State of the World's Children (UNICEF)
- Education for All (UNESCO)
- GenderStats database (World Bank).

Specific education indicators are defined as follows:[1]

Public expenditure on education. The percentage of GNP (Gross National Product) accounted for by public spending on public education plus subsidies to private education at the primary, secondary, and tertiary levels.

Expenditure per student, primary level. The total reported current spending by the government on primary education, divided by the total number of pupils in primary education, expressed as a percentage of per capita GNP.

Expenditure per student, secondary level. The total reported current spending by the government on secondary education, divided by the

---

[1] The definitions of indicators were developed by UNESCO and reported in the World Bank's GenderStats database: http://genderstats.worldbank.org/techEducation.htm (as of October 31, 2007).

total number of pupils in secondary education, expressed as a percentage of per capita GNP.

Female teachers (percentage of total). Full-time and part-time teachers.

Female pupils (percentage of total). Enrollments of girls in public and private schools.

Gross enrollment ratio. The ratio of total enrollment, regardless of age, to the population of the age group that officially corresponds to the level of education shown. Estimates are based on the International Standard Classification of Education (ICSED).

Net enrollment ratio. The ratio of the number of children of official school age (as defined by the national education system) who are enrolled in school to the population of the corresponding official school age.

Primary education. Education that provides children with basic reading, writing, and mathematics skills, along with an elementary understanding of such subjects as history, geography, natural science, social science, art, and music.

Secondary education. Education completing the basic education that began at the primary level, aimed at laying the foundations for life-long learning and human development by offering more subject- and skill-oriented instruction, using more-specialized teachers.

Children-out-of-school rate. The number of children of a given school age group who are not enrolled in school as a share of all children not enrolled.

Tertiary education. Education, whether or not to an advanced research qualification, that normally requires, as a minimum condition of admission, the successful completion of secondary-level education.

Progression to grade 5 (percentage of cohort reaching grade 5). The share of children enrolled in primary school who eventually reach grade 5. The estimate is based on the reconstructed cohort method.

Primary completion rate. The total number of students successfully completing (or graduating from) the last year of primary school in a given year, divided by the total number of children of official graduation age in the population. It follows the same methodology used by the Organisation for Economic Co-operation and Development

(OECD) for the calculation of secondary-school completion rates. The primary completion rate is a more comprehensive indicator of human-capital formation and school-system quality and efficiency than either gross or net enrollment ratios or the cohort survival rate, as it measures both education-system coverage and student attainment. It is also the most direct measure of national progress toward the Millennium Development Goal of universal primary completion. The primary completion rate is compiled by staff in the education group in the World Bank's Human Development Network.

Expected years of schooling. The average number of years of formal schooling that a child is expected to receive, including university education and years spent in repetition. The number is the sum of the underlying age-specific enrollment ratios for primary, secondary, and tertiary education.

Youth illiteracy rate (percentage of people 15–24 years of age). The percentage of people age 15 to 24 who cannot, with understanding, read and write a short, simple statement about their everyday life.

Health Indicators

Health statistics for the world's women are collected by the following organizations:

- United Nations Children's Fund (UNICEF) (www.unicef.org)
- The World's Women, United Nations Statistics Division (www.unstats.un.org)
- Progress of the World's Women 2002, United Nations Development Fund for Women (www.unifem.undp.org)
- Population and reproductive health country profiles, United Nations Population Fund (www.unfpa.org)
- World Health Organization (WHO): "Draft GWH Guidelines on Gender-Relevant Indicators in Health Research" (http://www.who.int/gender/documents/indicators/en/)
- WorldBank GenderStats database (http://genderstats.worldbank.org/home.asp).

Indicators of health, nutrition, and violence are defined as follows:[2]

Life expectancy at birth. The number of years a newborn infant would live if prevailing patterns of mortality at the time of its birth were to stay the same throughout its life. Data are from the World Bank's population database.

Child malnutrition. The percentage of children under five years of age whose weight for age is less than minus two standard deviations from the median for the international reference population ages 0 to 59 months. The reference population, selected by WHO in 1983, is based on children from the United States, who are assumed to be well nourished. Data have been compiled by World Bank staff from primary and secondary sources.

Child immunization rate. The percentage of children under one year of age receiving vaccination coverage for four diseases: measles, diphtheria, pertussis (whooping cough), and tetanus (DPT). A child is considered adequately immunized against measles after receiving one dose of vaccine and against DPT after receiving three doses. Data are from WHO and UNICEF.

Child mortality rate. The probability of dying between the ages of one and five. Data are from the Demographic and Health Surveys (DHS).

Maternal mortality rate. The number of women who die during pregnancy and childbirth per 100,000 live births. These data are estimates based on an exercise carried out by WHO and UNICEF in which maternal mortality was estimated with a regression model, using information on fertility, birth attendants, and HIV prevalence.

Births attended by skilled health staff. The percentage of deliveries attended by personnel trained to give the necessary supervision, care, and advice to women during pregnancy, labor, and the postpartum period; to conduct deliveries on their own; and to care for the newborn and infants. Data are from WHO and UNICEF.

---

[2] The definitions of indicators were developed by WHO and reported in the World Bank's GenderStats database: http://genderstats.worldbank.org/techHealth.html (as of October 2007).

Maternal leave benefits. The maternity benefits currently available to women in various countries. Data include information on the number of weeks of entitlement and the expected compensation during the covered period and are from the United Nations.

Prevalence of anemia (iron deficiency). Hemoglobin level less than 11 grams per deciliter in pregnant women. Data are from UNICEF.

Prevalence of HIV. The percentage of people 15 to 24 years of age who are infected with HIV. Data are from UNAIDS and the WHO AIDS Epidemic Update (2000).

Prevalence of physical violence against women. The percentage of adult women who have been physically assaulted by a current or former intimate partner—i.e., husband, boyfriend, or cohabiting partner—ever in any relationship. Refers only to physical violence.

Comparisons between studies must be made with caution because of the differences in definitions, sample sizes, data-collection approaches, and cultural factors between studies. As much as possible, data on health indicators are from studies based on representative samples of women. A few studies have national coverage, but most are limited to selected areas or cities. The information was self-reported by women and was gathered through face-to-face interviews, telephone interviews, or self-administered questionnaires. Some interviews were not conducted in private, which would inhibit women's ability to disclose violence by their partners. Data were compiled by WHO from existing studies.

Vital Governance Milestones for Afghan Women

Bonn Conference (November 27, 2001–December 5, 2002)

The Bonn conference will discuss the future of the Afghan nation, be they men or women. Although women's issues may not be covered, this meeting will decide the political future of Afghanistan, of which women are a part.[1]

—*Amena Afzali*

The Agreement on Provisional Arrangements in Afghanistan Pending the Reestablishment of Permanent Government Institutions

On November 27, 2001, the United Nations convened a conference in Bonn, Germany, to discuss the future of Afghanistan. These talks were the first since the end of the Taliban regime, and they brought together delegates from traditionally hostile ethnic factions to create a blueprint for an interim government. The following is an overview of the process. The four delegations that attended were the Northern Alliance, the "Rome group," the "Peshawar group," and the "Cypress group." The Northern Alliance, which controlled approximately half of the country at the time of the conference, sent a team comprising ethnic Tajiks, Uzbeks, Hazaras, and Pashtuns. It contributed 11 representatives to the discussion, two of whom were women. The Rome group, loyal to former King Mohammad Zaher Shah, who lives in exile in Rome and

---

[1] Benard et al., 2003.

did not attend the meeting, also contributed 11 representatives, one of whom was a woman. The Peshawar group, mostly Pashtun exiles based in Pakistan, contributed 5 representatives, one of whom was a woman. The Cypress group, exiles with ties to Iran, contributed 5 representatives, none of whom were women. It took convincing by the United Nations and the U.S. government to include women in the delegations.[2] According to The Advocacy Project,[3] a massive international lobbying effort secured the participation of women.[4] In addition to the delegations, 18 other countries sent representatives to monitor the talks.

The interim administration that was formed at the conference led the country for the next six months until the emergency meeting of the Loya Jirga in June of the following year. A timetable was set for this Loya Jirga, in turn, to pick a transitional administration that would run the country for the next two years, and the drafting of a new constitution to be approved by a Constitutional Loya Jirga. But the most difficult decisions made in Bonn were those on peacekeeping forces and a leader for the interim administration.

Interim Agreement (Signed on December 5, 2001)

The delegations agreed on an international peacekeeping force to be supervised by the United Nations. They selected Hamid Karzai to lead the country. Their goals in deciding the rest of the 29-member interim administration were to find an ethnic and political balance between representatives of the powerful Northern Alliance, the former king, and the two exile groups, and to secure a role for women.[5] The former king was given a largely symbolic role and was asked to convene the emergency meeting of the Loya Jirga in the spring. The Northern Alliance received about half of the seats in the interim cabinet, and members

---

[2] International Crisis Group, 2003.

[3] The Advocacy Project is a nonprofit organization that serves the needs of civil society—particularly community-based advocates for peace and human rights.

[4] AdvocacyNet, 2003.

[5] PBS, Frontline, "Filling the Vacuum: The Bonn Conference," http://www.pbs.org/wgbh/pages/frontline/shows/campaign/withus/cbonn.html.

of the Rome group were named to eight positions. One of the female Rome delegates, Sima Samar, was named Minister of Women's Affairs. Created as the interim government's first attempt to address women's issues, the ministry's mandate was to "support the government in reconciling to the needs and issues affecting women in all aspects of life to attain gender quality and full enjoyment of women's human rights and to ensure that Afghanistan's women's human rights and . . . legal, economic, social, political, and civic rights—including their right to be free from all forms of violence and discrimination—are respected, promoted, and fulfilled." Today, the Ministry of Women's Affairs has offices in 28 of the 34 provinces, and its budget for 2005–2006 was $1.5 million. One other woman joined the interim cabinet: Suhaila Seddiqi was named Minister of Public Health.

There were three categories of attendees at the Bonn Conference: delegates, alternates, and observers. Although four female representatives were present, only one of them—Amena Afzali of the Northern Alliance—served as a delegate. Another woman from the Northern Alliance, Seddiqa Balkhi, was an alternate. Sima Wali was an alternate for the Rome group; Fatima Gailani was an alternate for the Peshawar group; and Rona Mansuri was an observer from the Revolutionary Association of the Women of Afghanistan (RAWA) with the Rome group, put there as a result of pressure from the U.S. government.[6]

Sima Wali, the president of Refugee Women in Development, Inc.,[7] advocated the creation of the Ministry of Women's Affairs and the nomination of Sima Samar as one of the vice chairs of the interim authority.

According to Ishaq Nadiri,[8] one of the signatories of the Bonn Agreement, the vocal women at Bonn placed an emphasis on human

---

[6] Barnett Rubin, interview by Kathleen Lopez-Kim, June 21, 2003.

[7] Refugee Women in Development is an international nonprofit organization dedicated to the human rights and empowerment of women affected by civil strife and war.

[8] Ishaq Nadiri is a Jay Gould Professor of Economics at New York University, consultant to Hamid Karzai and the interim government in Afghanistan, and a participant in the Bonn talks, as well as in the Tokyo talks set up to attract international funding for Afghanistan's major reconstruction efforts.

rights and the notion of equality during the talks. At the same time, he observed that all those present had one main agenda: to create a road map for the progress of Afghanistan in all areas of life, including education, health care, gender equality, and work opportunities. To put this agenda in motion, they would first have to decide on an interim government. The female delegates wanted a representative government bound by the constitution and other laws, one that would best assist Afghanistan to move on from a history of conflict. When asked whether the number of female representatives present—only four out of a large group of mostly male delegates—was fair, Nadiri stated that because the conference was called in a short period of time, there was no notion of selection by quota, and therefore women were given as fair representation as was possible for the time. He asserted that the female delegates were free to make suggestions and were treated fairly by the male delegates, despite the need for some of them to adjust to the presence of women in a political process. Proof of this, he claims, is the creation of a ministry devoted solely to women's affairs for Afghanistan and its new cabinet.[9]

Professor Barnett Rubin,[10] a close advisor to Lakhdar Brahimi, the United Nations' special representative to Afghanistan, was present at the conference. His perception of the role of the women in Bonn was not as positive as Nadiri's. He observed:

> Like almost everyone else there, [the female delegates] played very little role in the actual negotiations. Sima Wali added the phrase "gender sensitive" to the preamble, but it was not discussed, since she said it in English and almost no one understood it. Amena Afzali objected to a phrase about representation in the Emergency Loya Jirga that put women with minorities, because they are not a minority. I cannot remember any other discussion of women. In general, most major issues were not discussed. The main issue

---

[9] Ishaq Nadiri, interview by Kathleen Lopez-Kim, June 18, 2003.

[10] Barnett Rubin helped to draft the Bonn Agreement. He is the director of studies at the Center on International Cooperation in New York University.

was the distribution of power among people represented there, not issues affecting the people of Afghanistan.[11]

Many women were not happy with the lack of female delegates at the Bonn Conference. Moreover, according to the Institute for Afghan Studies,[12] Amena Afzali is not popular with Afghan women because she had been living in Iran, and some felt she did not know about the suffering of the Afghan women. Some felt the presence of women was more symbolic to the international community than anything else. An international network, Women Living Under Muslim Laws (WLUML),[13] expressed concern to the United Nations about the lack of female delegates at Bonn:

> WLUML believes that international efforts for the reconstruction of Afghanistan must promote a process guided by the Afghan people. Afghan women are half of the Afghan people—a fact too often and too easily forgotten. It is not enough to call merely for the representation of various ethnic communities and/or factions in the decision making and transition processes around Afghanistan. The presence of Afghan civil society, most particularly women, at the negotiation table and decision making of any peace process is vital.[14]

In response to the desire of Afghan women to play a greater role in the reconstruction process, the United Nations Development Fund for Women (UNIFEM) organized a forum alongside the Bonn Conference, exclusively for the participation of Afghan women—those living in Afghanistan and those in the diaspora.

---

[11] Benard et al., 2003.

[12] The Institute for Afghan Studies (IAS) is a nonprofit, nonpolitical, independent center for research founded and run by young Afghan scholars from around the world.

[13] Women Living Under Muslim Laws is an international network that provides information, solidarity, and support for all women whose lives are shaped, conditioned, or governed by laws and customs said to derive from Islam.

[14] Women Living Under Muslim Laws, 2001.

Afghan Women's Summit for Democracy in Brussels (December 4–5, 2001)

> I have been in exile for a long time, and I was amazed at the resilience, intelligence, strength and ability of the Afghan women that I met who came from inside the country and all around the world. These women, I promise, can rebuild that country with no problem.[15]
>
> *—Zieba Shorish-Shamley*

The Afghan Women's Summit for Democracy in Brussels was held on December 4–5, 2001, during the time of the Bonn Conference. It was hosted by the European Women's Lobby, Equality Now, V-Day, the Center for Strategic Initiatives of Women, and the Feminist Majority in response to a request from women of Afghanistan for support and solidarity. It was coordinated by the Office of the Special Adviser on Gender Issues and Advancement of Women and UNIFEM. The result of the summit was the adoption of the Brussels Proclamation, which addresses women's demands with respect to the reconstruction of Afghanistan.

Zieba Shorish-Shamley, founder and director of the Women's Alliance for Peace and Human Rights in Afghanistan (WAPHA), was present at the Brussels Summit and observed that Afghan women were organized. They broke up into different groups that addressed topics such as human rights (Shorish-Shamley was a member of this group), health, the new constitution, education, and refugees. In these groups, Afghan women led the talks; the sponsors of the summit did not interfere with the process.[16] Shorish-Shamley also described the summit as a venting session: "The Summit was very important for providing a forum in which all the grievances of Afghan women in the country and in the diaspora could be expressed and heard. Mostly, women wanted basic rights such as access to healthcare and education for themselves and their children." After two days of discussion, the Brussels Proclamation

---

[15] Benard et al., 2003.

[16] Zieba Shorish-Shamley, interview by Kathleen Lopez-Kim, June 13, 2003.

was created, presented to the European Parliament, and then sent to the Bonn Conference mediator, Lakhdar Brahimi, and the president of the UN Security Council: "While the mostly male leaders in Germany have debated how to structure the new government of Afghanistan, the women in Belgium have set their agenda for what that government should do to restore women's rights and involve women in the political process."[17]

Some critics feel that events of this kind had symbolic character only and were a misallocation of resources. Shorish-Shamley, for example, stated, "They should have instead used the money for those who were dying of malnutrition. Rather than funds going to UNIFEM, more money should go to Afghan NGOs. A total of $900 million has been given to the UN. If Afghan women have to answer to so many bosses how can they have any empowerment?"[18]

Emergency Loya Jirga (June 10–16, 2002)

> I estimate that at least 80 percent of delegates favor excluding all warlords from the government. The 200 women delegates are especially outspoken on this issue. In a spontaneous display of democracy, they publicly rebuked two powerful symbols of Afghanistan's violent past—Burhannudin Rabbani, former President of the Mujahideen government from 1992–96, and Gen. Mohammed Fahim, former intelligence chief during this period and currently Defense Minister in the interim government. But due to behind-the-scenes pressure, our voices are being silenced and the warlords empowered.[19]
>
> —*Omar Zakhilwal*

The Emergency Loya Jirga, as prescribed under the Bonn Agreement, served the purpose of creating a transitional administration in Afghan-

---

[17] Janelle Brown, "Afghan Women's Summit," AlterNet, December 11, 2001. As of October 31, 2007: http://www.alternet.org/search_advanced.php.

[18] Benard et al., 2003.

[19] Zakhilwal, 2002.

istan to replace the interim government for up to two years until a fair, representative government could be chosen through democratic elections.

The process started when a special independent commission was appointed in January 2002. Its tasks were to establish rules and procedures for the Loya Jirga, to define a process for the selection of delegates, and to ensure adequate representation of women, minorities, religious scholars, representatives of civil-society groups, university faculty, trade groups, and other professionals. The commission released a set of rules and procedures in late March 2002.[20]

The next step, the selection process, started at the district level. First, groups of elders considered to represent the respected or powerful families in the region (*shuras*) met to pick electors, who would then go on to cast ballots for Loya Jirga delegates.[21] Each district chose a predetermined number of electors, based on the size of its population. Then, at regional observation centers, the electors were certified to cast ballots. They chose from among themselves a smaller number of Loya Jirga delegates, according to allotted numbers assigned to each district.

The Loya Jirga is a relatively representative process, but it is not fully democratic. This was particularly the case this time, due to the instability of the country and ongoing armed conflict:

> During the meetings, warlords not appointed to the assembly were allowed inside the tent where the Loya Jirga was in session, mingling with the delegates and threatening those who called for their exclusion or opposed their agenda. Several delegates, including some women, reported threats when they complained about the warlords' participation in the grand national assembly. Other delegates were alarmed at the heavy presence of agents from the Afghan Intelligence Service. A woman delegate, who asked to remain anonymous, told Human Rights Watch, "We are hostages

---

[20] Human Rights Watch, 2002b.

[21] The criteria for deciding who sits on these traditional leadership councils are complex and unwritten, and groups are often controlled by economically or militarily powerful forces in the region. As a result, political, gender-based, and ethnic inequalities are widespread.

of the people who destroyed Afghanistan. They [the warlords] are trying to hold us hostage to their power." Consistent with reports from many others, the delegate went on to describe efforts to coerce delegates. "There are petitions being circulated and we are pressed to just sign them without reading them, to agree with what is being said about who should be a candidate or chairman or have positions in the government. But we aren't given a chance to read these decisions, they just say 'sign it.'"[22]

Rasool Khawja, the founder of Herat Professional Shura,[23] was present at the Loya Jirga. He also agreed that it was not democratic: "The Loya Jirga was not controlled by the people. It was under the warlords' control."[24]

The assembly culminated in the election of the new transitional cabinet, named by Hamid Karzai, head of the transitional government. It differed only slightly from that of the interim administration.[25]

Few women were expected to be elected through the regular electoral process because of the traditional attitudes in Afghanistan constraining women from participating in political processes and security concerns inhibiting women from traveling to regional centers. However, 160 seats were guaranteed to women through appointment by the transitional government. Therefore, at least 11 percent of the seats were to go to women, although the Ministry of Women's Affairs called for 25 percent on International Women's Day, March 8, 2002.[26] A total of 1,051 delegates were selected by indirect district elections. Table B.1[27] shows the distribution of the appointed seats.

Many of the women at the assembly were trained teachers, doctors, and lawyers who were active in their own communities. Suraya

---

[22] Human Rights Watch, 2000.

[23] Herat Professional Association was established to aid in the reconstruction of Herat, a historic city in western Afghanistan.

[24] Rasool Khawja, interview by Kathleen Lopez-Kim, June 10, 2003.

[25] Human Rights News, 2002b.

[26] Benard et al., 2003.

[27] International Crisis Group, 2002, p. 7.

Table B.1
Distribution of Appointed Seats for the Emergency Loya Jirga

Participants	Total Number of Seats	Seats Reserved for Women
Members of the interim administration	30	2
Members of the Loya Jirga Commission	21	3
Religious personalities	6	0
Credible individuals	30	10
Civil-society members	51	12
Professional and scientific organizations	39	6
Nomads	25	0
Refugees	100[a]	25
Internally Displaced Persons	6	2
Other women from geographically distributed areas		100

[a]40 from Pakistan, 30 from Iran, and 30 from other countries.

Sadeed, founder and director of Help the Afghan Children (HTAC),[28] was one of the ten women present who were recognized nationally for their services. Sadeed was not particularly dissatisfied with the way the Loya Jirga turned out for women. She explained that it took place during the shock of change, and she decided not to complain about the presence of the warlords because things could have been worse. She believes that the single biggest achievement of the Loya Jirga is that over 1,300 Afghans from different factions, ethnicities, and backgrounds sat under one roof and behaved in a civilized manner. To have expected more was to have expected too much.[29]

Sadeed explained that in preparation for the meetings, the women congregated into different groups at night in the dormitories of a university compound where they slept. Some could not relate to each other because they had had such different experiences in life, but they all had the same goal: to give some type of legitimacy to the interim government. In other words, they were there to test whether Afghans were ready for democracy. Could a very conservative form of democracy

---

[28] HTAC is a U.S.-based nonprofit, nonpartisan, charitable organization established in 1993.

[29] Suraya Sadeed, interview by Kathleen Lopez-Kim, June 12, 2003.

be implemented after so many years of conflict? Though women did not have the concept of being one voice, they all wanted their desires to be heard, their groups to be noticed, and their grievances to be recognized.[30]

Sadeed also observed that the women at the Loya Jirga tended to bring attention to the basic needs of their own regions. They primarily asked for the right to education, security, work, and health care. Sadeed believes that Westerners' visions of a gender-equal society are at this early stage in the process different from what Afghan women envision:

> We need to understand that in the West, talking about women's rights is very legitimate. The women in Afghanistan are not ready—90 percent are illiterate. If we can implement the new constitution in just 50 percent of the country, it would be a very successful change. Afghans have a different state of mind than Westerners. Afghan women don't understand their basic rights like voting. They were taught to believe they are part of a society that belongs to men. The West should not compare or expect the same results as far as women's rights go. Human rights should be within the context of that culture. Why? Society is not ready for it—it is occupied with today's problems. Why do women wear the burqa still? Because 98 percent are impoverished and they want to remain anonymous as beggars.[31]

Heather Fortuna, of Women for Women International, observed that there are women in Afghanistan who want to be involved in the political process, and there are women who are more concerned with their own family. The political interest of women depends on the socioeconomic class they belong to.[32]

Ishaq Nadiri, who was also present at the Loya Jirga, claims that it was a success for women, because more than 10 percent of the delegates were women. He pointed out that one of them even ran for president

---

[30] Benard et al., 2003.

[31] Ibid.

[32] Heather Fortuna, interview by Kathleen Lopez-Kim, June 11, 2003.

and gave a very stimulating speech. The women were as active as the men. They pushed for equality before the law and demanded the same rights as men. They were especially concerned about widows, women's health, and education. The attitude of the male delegates showed that the involvement of women in a political process was something new to them that they would have to get used to, but there was no hostility. The warlords did not pose a threat. The women were extremely keen about asking questions and were vigorous participants.[33]

Shorish-Shamley, also present at the Loya Jirga, found cause for optimism in the meetings as well, especially in the fact that a large group of Afghans gathered without killing each other. Similar to the Bonn Conference, she described it as "a healing process to talk about grievances."[34]

Shorish-Shamley was also aware of the presence of militias and predicted that lack of security would, unfortunately, be a great problem at the Constitutional Loya Jirga as well.[35]

Constitutional Drafting and Review Commissions (October 2002)

President Karzai on October 5, 2002, established a nine-member Drafting Commission which was charged with the task of drafting a new constitution. The commission included two women, Asifa Kakar and Mukarama Akrami, both former students of Vice President Shahrani at Kabul University. Kakar, a lawyer by training, worked in Peshawar, where she taught civil and Shari'a law at a university, while Akrami holds a bachelor's degree in Islamic Law from Kabul University and was at the time a member of the Kabul High Court in the commercial division. Of her role on the commission, Kakar had the following to say: "I am one of the first women to ever be part of drafting a constitution in the history of my country. My first feeling was one of excite-

---

[33] Benard et al., 2003.

[34] Ibid.

[35] Ibid.

ment to realize that this opportunity exists for women. But I also had many worries as I realized what a critical role I had. I felt responsible to all my people, especially women."[36]

The first draft was presented to President Karzai in March 2003. The Drafting Commission was then replaced by a 35-member Review Commission in May 2003. This new commission, which includes seven women, was created to assist with the education and public information campaigns for informing the greater public about the constitutional process. To do so, they utilized focus groups, bringing together like-minded Afghans in thematic groups, such as youth, elders, Islamic scholars, women, and NGO representatives. While the process was highly unscientific, it yielded some important conclusions regarding people's concerns over the constitutional process and result.

The Review Commission was also tasked with presenting the final document for ratification at a 25-day-long Constitutional Loya Jirga to be held in October 2003.[37]

The mandate of the Constitutional Commission states that:

The Commission will *ensure broad participation of women* in the constitution-making process. The Constitutional Drafting Commission consists *of nine members including two women.* The representation of women will increase in the soon to be established Commission. The women commissioners will lead, where possible, consultations with women in light of culture sensitivities in some areas. The Commission will also educate the public through their regional and provincial staff to inform women and other groups about the need for women's involvement in the process. The staff will also identify suitable venues, times and ways of meeting and/or communicating with the Commission.

The Commission will be working closely with the Ministry of Women's Affairs, which together with UNIFEM, is collecting inputs, holding seminars and other public education programs about the constitutional rights of women. Further, the Commis-

---

[36] Heyzer, 2004.

[37] Benard et al., 2003.

sion will liaise with the women civil society organizations that will put at the disposal of the Commission a broad network of their grass root organizations. Gender balance is also a priority for the selection of the regional consultation teams.

Both the Constitutional Commission and the Review Commission encountered sharp critiques of the mandate as expressed in the constitution and the information collected for its rewrite. There was also sharp criticism of the fact that focus groups met without release of a draft constitution and thus were mostly for show. In addition, security concerns were problematic in many provinces, keeping the southern parts of the country muted in the discourse process.

Additionally, international groups called on the commissions to work to better integrate women into the text of the constitution, calling for inclusion of provisions to guarantee women's rights in crisis situations, to ensure citizenship, to implement legal renderings regarding the age of marriage, to implement rules for compulsory education for girls and boys, and to clarify issues regarding Islamic law and international women's rights.

Constitutional Loya Jirga (December 2003–January 2004)

We have to struggle to maintain a bright future for millions of women suffering from violence, ultraconservatism, illiteracy, maternal mortality and many other deprivations. I am really proud of being a part of the Loya Jirga as it has great historic value, and after years of misery and disorder, Afghans, both men and women, have at last come together peacefully to achieve some kind of progress.[38]

—*Delegate Sa'era Sharif*

The Constitutional Loya Jirga was assembled in late 2003 to review and adapt the constitution drafted by the Constitutional Commission.

---

[38] Interview in "Integrated Regional Information Network (IRIN) News: Afghanistan," http://www.irinnews.org/report.asp?ReportID=38522&SelectRegion=Central_Asia.

Unlike the Emergency Loya Jirga, the Constitutional Loya Jirga consisted of more than 20 percent women (166 delegates out of 500) and relied partly on presidential appointments for its delegates. In addition to endorsing the constitution, this group was responsible for codifying the presidential and legislative systems, a task that was carried out under the auspices of a high value on human rights. It was at the Constitutional Loyal Jirga that the international security assistance forces gained permission for deployment and the construction of a national army began.

However, not all of the proceedings went smoothly. Former warlords were successful at imbedding themselves in the process, due to long-standing tribal and familial bonds. This introduced the idea that women delegates at the actual event might receive threats of harm or actual harm. It also created tension surrounding the issue of whether or not a specific clause would be dedicated to the exclusion of the Taliban within the state infrastructure. Similar to the model of post–World War II Germany, such a clause would effectively terminate any ability of the remaining members to regroup and rearm themselves. However, the clause was not included in the constitution, and today its absence is often linked to the resurgence of this once powerful group of criminals that was so detrimental to the lives of women.

The issue of gendered representation also took center stage at the Loya Jirga, as every step represented a great fight for the continued preservation and inclusion of women's rights. Midway through the event, several women's groups organized protests out of concern for highly biased language regarding gendered rights in the proposed constitution. They feared that the constitution did not have any language regarding the internal ability of Islam and its role in women's property, marriage, and protection rights. Despite the difficulty, the delegates came to consensus and endorsed the constitution on January 4, 2004.

Many felt that both the number of women present and the amount of attention their events received were very limited. While the Beijing Declaration and Security Council Resolution 1325 both call for high representation of women, the actual number was disproportionately lower than the population ratio. Further, women's-rights issues were highly marginalized during the event, cited as part of a Western agenda, and used as a piece of propaganda to link advocates to anti-religious values.[39]

It is vital to consider here the selection process for the participants in the Loya Jirga. Of the 500 members of this body, 450 should be elected and 50 should be appointed by the president. Of those elected, 64 must be women; of those appointed, 25 should be women (a combined 20 percent of the total seats). The Bonn Commission also set forth principles for managing the selection of individuals to the body:

1. Election of members of the Loya Jirga to approve the constitution must take place in a just and open atmosphere free of any interference, trouble, political influence, and national and regional tendencies.
2. Patriotism, national unity, and the interest of the Afghan people are to be considered basic criteria.
3. The electorates must try to elect educated people with sufficient influence who must have basic knowledge of the principles of the constitution.[40]

These criteria, while helpful, promoted a vague idea of what kinds of people should make up this important body. Feeling that women were overshadowed by the role of "influential" actors, advocacy groups and NGOs worked to ensure that their issues would receive adequate attention at the event.

One of the most controversial parts of the Loya Jirga occurred when Delegate Malalai Joya, an elected representative of Farah Province who was a social worker involved in establishing an orphanage and a health clinic, spoke out against the inclusion of warlords and the lack of women representatives. Her comments, which lasted three minutes, were emotionally charged and highly influential: "I feel pity and I feel very sorry that those who call Loya Jirja an infidel basis equivalent to blasphemy after coming here their words are accepted, or please see the committees and what people are whispering about. The

---

[39] Brunet and Helal, 2003.

[40] Ibid.

chairman of every committee is already selected. Why do you not take all these criminals to one committee so that we see what they want for this nation? These were those who turned our country into the nucleus of national and international wars. They were the most anti-women people in the society who wanted to [makes pause] who brought our country to this state and they intend to do the same again. I believe that it is a mistake to test those already being tested. They should be taken to national and international court. If they are forgiven by our people, the bare-footed Afghan people, our history will never forgive them. They are all recorded in the history of our country."[41] Joya was expelled from the session. After surviving numerous assassination attempts, the first occurring in the few seconds after her speech, Joya lives today in Afghanistan, where she is a representative to parliament and a constant source of discourse and debate regarding women's issues.

Following the Constitutional Loya Jirga, the highly influential RAWA issued the following statement: "The fake nature of the Constitutional Loya Jirga and freedom of speech were clear to all the people of Afghanistan and the world. . . . We now have a constitution that has nothing to guarantee the trial of warlord criminals, allows the misuse of religion, and has not abolished the various crimes against women in the name of religion and tradition. The Constitution is just a piece of paper that gives legitimacy to the tyrannical rule of warlords."

Presidential Election (September 2004)

Originally scheduled for June 2004, the election of September 2004 was run by a joint UN-assisted mission in Afghanistan and Afghanistan Electoral Body partnership. There were a total of 10.5 million registered voters, and 8 million votes were cast (an 80 percent turnout). Voting was conducted on a district-based voting scale, rather than proportional voting. Besides Hamid Karzai, who had commanded the interim government, there were 15 candidates, the most serious chal-

---

[41] This quotation was translated from the Dari language. Some of the wording seems odd, but it is taken directly from the translation.

lenger being education minister Yunis Qanooni. One woman ran for this position, Masooda Jalal. She later became a member of the Loya Jirga. Roughly 9,000 NATO-trained forces were on staff to increase the security level. Some 400 national voting observers were organized by the Organization for Security and Cooperation in Europe. International donations amounted to $90 million, roughly half of which was from the United States.[42]

Parliamentary Elections (September 2005)

The parliamentary elections of 2005 were originally scheduled by the Bonn Agreement for 2004, in tandem with the presidential election. However, Afghanistan officials realized that this timeline was much too short and thus rescheduled them, once for February 2005 and again for later in the year. These elections were for the Wolesi Jirga (the legislative national assembly), along with the provincial councils. The time frame for these elections was very short, and a difficult security environment created complications for the planning committees. However, 6 million Afghans voted in the elections, 44 percent of whom were women. Political parties were effectively mainstreamed into the election process, along with an increase in the reliability of institutions.

The major controversy for these elections was the arrival of more than 5,000 registered complaints. Even with the newly created Joint Electoral Management Body (JEMB), the infrastructure to deal with so many complaints did not exist. However, an international commission of more than 90,000 election observers was on hand to help deal with the problems.

The London Conference on Afghanistan (January 31–February 1, 2006)

Sixty international delegations met in London under the auspices of the United Nations to discuss the conclusion of the Bonn Conference

---

[42] Katzman, 2006.

and the remaining goals for Afghanistan. Their focus was on four main topics: security, governance, reconstruction and development, and counternarcotics. The event focused on the continued and sustained participation of the donor community and the high reliance on this community. The United States promised another $1.1 billion in reconstruction funding so that Afghanistan could enter what U.S. Secretary of State Condoleezza Rice called "a new stage of development." Rice further stated, "We will have a chance to celebrate how much progress Afghanistan has made since the dark days when the Taliban ruled and oppressed the people of Afghanistan to the election of you [Karzai] as President and then as a freely elected parliament. It is quite a wonderful story and it is testament to the spirit of the Afghan people and their desire for liberty."[43]

The result of the London Conference was the Afghanistan Compact, an outline for the way forward in Afghanistan. This document serves as an agreement regarding the commitment of the government of Afghanistan and the international community to continue to establish those social institutions that will bring about a peaceful and secure future for the Afghan people. Additionally, it works to implement a system that would encourage growth and sustainable economic and social development within the nation. The only explicit mention of women in the compact came under the heading "Goal of Social Protection," listed under the heading "Security." The compact commits to the proposition that "by the end of 2010 the number of female headed households that are poor will be reduced by 20 percent and employment rates will increase by 20 percent."[44] However, less explicitly, the document makes several statements regarding the importance of increasing security—an issue that has negatively affected women's ability to obtain the rights delegated to them by the constitution.

RAWA had the following to say regarding the London Conference on Afghanistan: "While another 10 billion were pledged at the recent London conference, even a fraction of this aid has not been used for the benefit and welfare of our people, but filled the pockets of the

---

[43] U.S. Department of State, 2006.

[44] Afghanistan Compact, 2006.

warlords and high rank officials. According to Dr. Ramadan Bashar Dost, a popular MP and former minister of planning, if 1 billion of the aid reaching Afghanistan was spent honestly to benefit people, Afghanistan's features would have changed."[45]

---

[45] Rawi, 2006.

National Solidarity Program Case-Study Survey

As part of the National Solidarity Program (NSP) case study, a seven-question email survey and a data sheet were sent to all 24 facilitating partners (FPs). Twenty-one of the FPs provided some form of response to this initial request for information. Three FPs (the Norwegian Project Office–Rural Rehabilitation Association (NPO/RRA), Relief International (RI), and ZOA Refugee Care) were in very early stages of program implementation and thus were not in a position to respond. RI did, however, provide information on its number of female staff members. One FP declined to participate due to staff time constraints. Thirteen of the FPs responded to the questions, and 13 provided the requested data.

The Questionnaire

The questionnaire asked the following questions:

1. What challenges have you faced in including women in NSP (as implementers, participants, and beneficiaries)?
2. What steps have you taken to overcome these challenges?
3. How do you work around potential constraints against the active participation of women in the CDCs? (If mixed CDCs, how is female attendance and active participation facilitated? If female-only CDCs are used, how are the priorities, ideas, opinions, and proposed projects communicated and coordinated with the male-only CDC?)

4. How has the participation of women in NSP changed during the life of the program?
5. What, if any, gender training does your staff receive?
6. What, if any, gender-mainstreaming actions does your organization employ?
7. What, if any, success stories do you have regarding the role of women in nation-building through NSP?

The Data Sheet

The following data were requested:

FP staffing
- Number of field office staff
- Number of females in field office staff
- Number of social organizers (SOs)
- Number of female SOs
- Number of district-level staff
- Number of female district-level staff
- Number of province-level staff
- Number of female province-level staff
- Number of country and headquarter NSP staff
- Number of female country and headquarter NSP staff

CDCs
- Number of CDCs in all participating communities
- Number of mixed male/female CDCs
- Number of female-only CDCs
- Number of male-only CDCs
- Number of females in all participating communities
- Number of males in all participating communities
- Number of females who voted in CDC elections
- Number of males who voted in CDC elections
- Number of CDC elections for males only
- Number of CDC elections for women only

- Total number of representatives for mixed CDCs
- Total number of female representatives for mixed CDCs
- Total number of male representatives for mixed CDCs
- Total number of officers for mixed CDCs
- Total number of male officers for mixed CDCs
- Total number of female officers for mixed CDCs
- Number of female members of mixed CDCs who attend meetings
- Number of female members of mixed CDCs who actively participate in meetings
- Total number of representatives for male CDCs
- Total number of representatives for female CDCs

Community Development Plans
- Number of community development projects
- Total amount of funding for community development projects
- Number of community development projects targeting women specifically
- Total amount of funding for community development projects targeting women specifically
- Total number of community development projects proposed by female CDCs
- Total number of community development projects proposed by female CDCs that are being or have been implemented

Bibliography

"ABC News Poll: Life in Afghanistan," New York: ABC News, 2005.

Abirafeh, Lina, "Lessons from Gender Focused International Aid in Post-Conflict Afghanistan . . . Learned?" *Gender and International Cooperation 7*, Bonn: Friedrich-Ebert-Stiftun, 2005. As of October 29, 2007:
http://www.eldis.org/static/DOC20470.htm

AdvocacyNet, *The Women of Kosovo and Afghanistan Pledge Solidarity with Iraqi Women*, The Advocacy Project, News Bulletin No. 5, May 2003. As of October 29, 2007:
http://.advocacynet.org/resource/751

Afghan Interim Administration, *National Development Framework*, Kabul, 2002.

Afghan Women's Network, web site. As of October 29, 2007:
http://www.afghanwomensnetwork.org/index.php?q=node/

The Afghanistan Compact, London Conference on Afghanistan, January 31, 2006. As of October 29, 2007:
http://www.fco.gov.uk/servlet/Front?pagename=OpenMarket/Xcelerate/ShowPage&c=Page&cid=1132599286730

Afghanistan Research and Evaluation Unit (AREU), "Lessons from Approaches to Increase Women's Participation in Development: Workshop Summary," March 2005. As of October 29, 2007:
www.areu.org.af/index.php?option=com_docman&task=doc_view&gid=39

Afghanistan State Government, Ministry of Rural Rehabilitation, *Development Newsletter*, Vol. 1, No. 4, July 2004.

Afshar, Haleh, and Deborah Eade (eds.), *Development, Women, and War: Feminist Perspectives*, London: Oxfam Publishing, 2004.

Ahern, Patricia, Paul Nuti, and Julia M. Masterson, "Promoting Gender Equity in the Democratic Process: Women's Paths to Political Participation and Decision-making," Washington, DC: The International Center for Research on Women, 2001. As of October 29, 2007:
http://www.icrw.org/docs/GCSLsynthesispaper.pdf#search=%22Promoting%20Gender%20Equity%20in%20the%20Democratic%20Process%3A%20Women's%20Paths%20to%20Political%20Participation%20and%20Decision-making%22

Aikman, Sheila, and Elaine Unterhalter (eds.), *Beyond Access: Transforming Policy and Practice for Gender Equality in Education*, Oxford, UK: OXFAM Publishing, 2005. As of October 25, 2007:
http://publications.oxfam.org.uk/oxfam/add_info_010.asp

Alkire, Sabina, "Conceptual Framework for Human Security," Oxford, UK: University of Oxford, Centre for Research on Inequality, Human Security and Ethnicity, CRISE, 2003. As of October 29, 2007:
http://www.crise.ox.ac.uk/pubs/workingpaper2.pdf

Amnesty International, Afghanistan, *Killing of Safiye Amajan Violates Laws of War and Signals Need for Protection of Activists*, New York: Amnesty International, 2006.

———, "Afghanistan: Addressing the Past to Secure the Future," New York, April 7, 2005a. As of November 4, 2007:
http://web.amnesty.org/library/Index/ENGASA110032005

———, "Afghanistan: Women Still Under Attack: A Systematic Failure to Protect," May 30, 2005b. As of November 4, 2007:
http://web.amnesty.org/library/Index/ENGASA110072005

———, "Afghanistan: Women Failed by Progress in Afghanistan," New York, October 28, 2004a. As of November 4, 2007:
http://news.amnesty.org/index/ENGASA110152004

———, *Casualties of War, Women's Bodies Women's Lives*, Amnesty Publications, 2004b.

———, "Security Council Resolution 1325: History and Analysis," 2004c. As of November 4, 2007:
http://www.peacewomen.org/un/anniversaryindex.html

———, "No One Listens to Us and No One Treats Us as Human Beings: Justice Denied to Women," New York, 2003.

———, "Pakistan: Honour Killings of Girls and Women," AI Index, ASA 33/018/1999, September 1999a.

———, "Women in Afghanistan: Pawns in Men's Power Struggles," New York, 1999b.

——, "International Criminal Court Fact Sheet, Number 7: Ensuring Justice for Women." As of November 4, 2007:
http://www.amnestyusa.org/icc/document.
do?id=962E12D23AAB025080256FC700373120

Amowitz, Lynn L., Vincent Iacopino, Holly Burkhalter, Sandhya Gupta, and Alicia Ely-Yamin, "Women's Health and Human Rights in Afghanistan: A Population-Based Assessment," Cambridge, MA: Physicians for Human Rights, August 2001.

Ampofo, Akosua, Josephine Bettes, Wairmu Njambi, and Mary Osirim, "Women and Gender Studies in English Speaking Sub Saharan Africa: A Review of Research in the Social Sciences," *Gender and Society*, Vol. 18, No. 6, 2004, pp. 685–714.

Anderlini, Sanam, *Women at the Peace Table: Making a Difference*, New York: United Nations Press, 2000.

Anderlini, Sanam Naraghi, Camille Pampell Conaway, and Lisa Keys, "Justice, Governance and Civil Society," in Women Waging Peace, *Inclusive Security, Sustainable Peace: A Toolkit for Advocacy and Action*, London: International Alert, and Washington, DC: Women Waging Peace, 2004.

Anwer, Syed, "Locked-up Afghans Lured by Drug Mafia," *The Frontier Post*, August 27, 2001.

Aruna, Rao, Mary Anderson, and Catherine Overholt, *Gender Analysis in Development Planning*, West Hartford, CT: Kumarian Press, 1991.

Asia Foundation, *Democracy in Afghanistan. 2004: A Survey of the Afghanistan Electorate*, 2004. As of November 4, 2007:
http://www.asiafoundation.org/pdf/afghan_voter-ed04.pdf

Asian Development Bank and World Bank, *Afghanistan: Preliminary Needs Assessment for Recovery and Reconstruction*, German Federal Ministry of the Interior, Kabul, January 2002.

Azarbaijani-Moghadam, Sippi, "Afghan Women on the Margins of the Twenty First Century," in Antonio Donini et al., *Nation-Building Unraveled: Aid Peace and Justice in Afghanistan*, Bloomfield, CT: Kumarian Press, Inc., 2004.

Bajpai, Kanti, *Human Security: Concept and Measurement*, Notre Dame, IN: Joan B. Kroc Institute for International Peace Studies, Occasional Paper No. 19, OP 1, August 2000. As of November 4, 2007:
http://kroc.nd.edu/ocpapers/op_19_1.PDF

Bannon, Ian, *Gender and Post-Conflict Reconstruction: The World Bank Track Record*, Washington, DC: Heinrich Böll Foundation/Brookings Institution, 2004.

Barakat, Sultan, and Gareth Wardell, "Exploited by Whom? An Alternative Perspective on Humanitarian Assistance to Afghan Women," *Third World Quarterly*, Vol. 23, No. 5, 2002, pp. 909–930.

_____ , "Capitalizing on Capacities of Afghan Women: Women's Role in Afghanistan's Reconstruction and Development," Geneva: In-focus Program on Crisis Response and Reconstruction, Working Paper No. 4, 2001.

BBC News, "Profile: Malalai Joya," November 2005a. As of November 4, 2007: http://news.bbc.co.uk/2/hi/south_asia/4420832.stm

_____ , "Q&A: Afghan Election Guide," October 2005b. As of October 29, 2007: http://news.bbc.co.uk/1/hi/world/south_asia/4251580.stm

Benard, Cheryl, _Our Country, My Role: Supporting the Participation of Afghanistan's Women in Political and Civic Society_, Vienna, Austria: Women Without Borders, 2005. As of November 4, 2007: http://afghanistan.unfpa.org/Docs/Our%20Country%20My%20Role%20Englis h.pdf

Benard, Cheryl, and Nina Hachigian (eds.), _Democracy and Islam in the New Constitution of Afghanistan_, Santa Monica, CA: RAND Corporation, CF-186/1-CAPP, 2003. As of October 25, 2007: http://www.rand.org/pubs/conf_proceedings/CF186.1/

Benard, Cheryl, Edith Schlaffer, Kathleen Kim-Lopez, and Martina Handler, "Strategies for Women's Participation in Afghan Nation-Building from Bonn to Pre-Election," German Federal Ministry of the Interior, Zwischenbericht Jubiläumsfondprojekt Nr. 9723, July 2003.

Bergen, Peter, "Waltzing with Warlords," _The Nation_, January 1, 2007. As of November 5, 2007: http://www.lawandsecurity.org/get_article/?id=60

Berntsen, Gary, and Ralph Pezzullo, _Jawbreaker: The Attack on Bin Laden and Al Qaeda_, New York: Crown Publishers, 2005.

Bhatia, Michael, Kevin Lanigan, and Philip Wilkinson, _Minimal Investments, Minimal Results: The Failure of Security Policy in Afghanistan_, Kabul: Afghanistan Research and Evaluation Unit, AREU Briefing Paper, June 2004.

Biddle, Stephen, _Afghanistan and the Future of Warfare: Implications for Army and Defense Policy_, Carlisle, PA: Strategic Studies Institute, U.S. Army War College, November 2002.

Boesen, Inger, "From Subjects to Citizens: Local Participation in the National Solidarity Programme," Afghanistan Research and Evaluation Unit, August 2004. As of November 5, 2007: http://topics.developmentgateway.org/afghanistan/rc/ItemDetail. do~1011063?itemId=1011063

Borders, Robert, "Provincial Reconstruction Teams in Afghanistan: A Model for Post-Conflict Reconstruction and Development," _Journal of Development and Social Transformation_, Vol. 1, November 2004.

Brown, Janelle, "Afghan Women's Summit," AlterNet, December 11, 2001. As of November 5, 2007:
www.alternet.org

Brunet, Ariane, and Isabelle Solon Helal, "Seizing an Opportunity: Afghan Women and the Constitution Making Process," *Rights and Democracy Mission Report*, Quebec, Canada: International Center for Human Rights and Democratic Development, May 2003.

Buffaloe, David L., *Conventional Forces in Low-Intensity Conflict: The 82d Airborne in Firebase Shkin*, Arlington, VA: Association of the United States Army, Landpower Essay 04-2, 2004.

Bushra, Judy, Ancil Adrian-Paul, and Maria Olson, "Women Building Peace: Sharing Know How, Assessing Impact, Planning for Miracles," *International Alert*, London, June 2005. As of November 5, 2007:
http://www.international-alert.org/publications/121.php

Byrne, Bridget, "Towards a Gendered Understanding of Conflict, Section 2: Workbook Readings," *IDS Bulletin*, No. 27, Brighton, UK: University of Sussex, Institute of Development Studies, 1996.

Callamard, Agnes, et al., *Investigating Women's Rights Violations in Armed Conflicts*, Amnesty International Publications, with the International Centre for Human Rights and Democratic Development, Canada, 2001.

Caprioli, Mary, "Primed for Violence: The Role of Gender Inequality in Predicting Internal Conflict," *International Studies Quarterly*, Vol. 49, 2005, pp. 161–178.

——, "Democracy and Human Rights Versus Women's Security: A Contradiction?" *Security Dialogue*, Vol. 35, No. 4, 2004, pp. 411–428. As of November 5, 2007:
http://sdi.sagepub.com/cgi/reprint/35/4/411

——, "Gender Equality and State Aggression: The Impact of Domestic Gender Equality on State First Use of Force," *International Interactions*, Vol. 29, 2003, pp. 195–214.

Caprioli, Mary, and Mark Boyer, "Gender, Violence, and International Crisis," *Journal of Conflict Resolution*, Vol. 45, No. 4, August 2001, pp. 503–518.

Carment, David, Souleima el Achkar, Stewart Prest, and Yiagadeesen Samy, "The 2006 Country Indicators for Foreign Policy: Opportunities and Challenges for Canada," *Canadian Foreign Policy*, Vol. 13, No. 1, 2006, pp. 1–35.

Carroll, Jill, "Iraqi Women Eye Islamic Law," *The Christian Science Monitor*, June 2006. As of November 5, 2007:
http://www.csmonitor.com/2005/0225/p07s02-woiq.html

Chamlou, Nadereh, "Gender and Development in the Middle East and North Africa—Women in the Public Sphere," presentation to the Woodrow Wilson International Center for Scholars, Middle East Program, Washington, DC, January 2004. As of November 5, 2007:
http://wilsoncenter.org/index.cfm?fuseaction=events.
event_summary&event_id=54315

Chiarelli, Major General Peter, "Winning the Peace: The Requirement for Full Spectrum Operations," *Military Review*, July 2005.

Cohn, Carol, and Cynthia Enloe, "A Conversation with Cynthia Enloe, Feminists Look at Masculinity and the Men Who Wage War," *Signs: Journal of Women in Culture and Society*, Vol. 28, No. 5, The University of Chicago, 2003.

Coleman, Isobel, "Beyond the Burqa," *Georgetown Journal of International Affairs*, Summer/Fall 2004a. As of November 5, 2007:
http://journal.georgetown.edu/Issues/sf04/CulSoc%20Coleman.pdf

——, "The Payoff from Women's Rights," *Foreign Affairs,* Vol. 83, No. 3, June 2004b, pp. 80–95.

——, "Post-Conflict Reconstruction: The Importance of Women's Participation in Afghanistan and Iraq," Testimony Before the Congressional Human Rights Caucus, United States Congress, Washington, DC, March 11, 2004c. As of November 5, 2007:
http://www.cfr.org/publication/6909/postconflict_reconstruction.html

Coleman, Isobel, and Swanee Hunt, "Afghanistan Should Make Room for Its Female Leaders: Denying Women Positions of Influence Is Fundamentally Undemocratic," *The Christian Science Monitor*, April 24, 2006. As of November 5, 2007:
http://www.csmonitor.com/2006/0424/p09s01-coop.html

Commission on Human Security, *Human Security Now: Final Report*, 2003. As of November 5, 2007:
http://www.humansecurity-chs.org/finalreport/index.html

Conaway, Camille P., *The Role of Women in Stabilization and Reconstruction*, Stabilization and Reconstruction Series, Washington, DC: United States Institute of Peace. As of November 5, 2007:
http://www.usip.org/pubs/specialreports/srs/srs_three.pdf#search=%22The%20Rol
e%20of%20Women%20in%20Stabilization%20and%20Reconstruction%2C%20
Stabilization%20and%20Reconstruction%20Series%22

Conaway, Camille P., and Salome Martinez, *Adding Value: Women's Contributions to Reintegration and Reconstruction in El Salvador*, Cambridge, MA, and Washington, DC: Women Waging Peace, January 2004. As of November 5, 2007:
http://www.womenwagingpeace.net/content/articles/ElSalvadorExecSummary.pdf

"Country Risk Assessment: Afghanistan," *Jane's Intelligence Review*, Vol. 16, No. 5, May 2004, pp. 38–41.

Coursen-Neff, Zama, "The Taliban's War on Education," *Los Angeles Times*, July 31, 2006, p. 11.

Courtney, Morgan, et al., *In the Balance: Measuring Progress in Afghanistan*, Washington, DC: Center for Strategic and International Studies, 2005.

Cunningham, Karla J., "Women, Political Violence and Democratization," in William Crotty (ed.), *Democratic Development and Political Terrorism*, Boston, MA: Northeastern University Press, 2005.

Danish Immigration Service, *Political Conditions, Security, and Human Rights Situation in Afghanistan*, Report of Fact-Finding Mission to Islamabad and Peshawar, Pakistan, and Kabul, Afghanistan, 2002.

Davis, Anthony, "Afghan Security Deteriorates as Taliban Regroup," *Jane's Intelligence Review*, Vol. 15, No. 5, May 2003.

——— , "Kabul's Security Dilemma," *Jane's Defence Weekly*, Vol. 37, No. 24, June 12, 2002.

Department for International Development, United Kingdom, "Conducting Conflict Assessments: Guidance Notes," January 2002. As of November 5, 2007: http://www.dfid.gov.uk/pubs/files/conflictassessmentguidance.pdf

Derbyshire, Helen, *Gender Manual: A Practical Guide for Development Policy Makers and Practitioners*, Department for International Development, United Kingdom, April 2002. As of November 5, 2007: http://www.dfid.gov.uk/pubs/files/gendermanual.pdf

Dobbins, James, Seth G. Jones, Keith Crane, and Beth Cole DeGrasse, *The Beginners Guide to Nation-Building*, Santa Monica, CA: RAND Corporation, MG-557-SRF, 2007. As of November 5, 2007: http://www.rand.org/pubs/monographs/MG557/

Dobriansky, Paula, "Commemoration of the Passage of the 19th Amendment," U.S. Department of State, August 24, 2006. As of November 5, 2007: http://www.state.gov/g/rls/rm/71867.htm

Dollar, David, Raymond Fismond, and Roberta Gatti, *Are Women Really the 'Fairer Sex'? Corruption and Women in Government*, Washington, DC: The World Bank, Policy Research Report on Gender and Development, Working Paper Series No. 4, 1999. As of November 5, 2007: http://siteresources.worldbank.org/INTGENDER/Resources/wp4.pdf

Donini, Antonio, et al., *Nation-Building Unraveled: Aid, Peace and Justice in Afghanistan*, Bloomfield, CT: Kumarian Press, Inc., 2004.

Dupree, Nancy Hatch, "Afghan Women Under the Taliban," in William Maley (ed.), *Fundamentalism Reborn? Afghanistan and the Taliban,* New York: New York University Press, 1998.

Enloe, Cynthia, *The Morning After: Sexual Politics at the End of the Cold War,* Los Angeles, CA: University of California Press, 1993.

——, *Bananas, Beaches, and Bases: Making Feminist Sense of International Politics,* Los Angeles, CA: University of California Press, 1990.

Esfandiari, Golnaz, "Afghanistan, Self Immolation of Women on the Rise in Western Provinces," Radio Free Europe, March 1, 2004. As of November 5, 2007: http://www.rferl.org/featuresarticle/2004/03/ea74ad8e-9b91-4cbd-b7f7-f13b521dce2b.html

Farr, Vanessa, "The Importance of a Gender Perspective to Successful Disarmament Demobilization and Reintegration Process," UNIFEM Disarmament Forum, United Nations, 2003. As of December 13, 2007: http://www.unidir.org/pdf/articles/pdf-art1995.pdf

Fearon, James D., and David D. Laitin, "Ethnicity, Insurgency, and Civil War," *American Political Science Review,* Vol. 97, No. 1, February 2003.

Fox, Mary Jane, "Girl Soldiers: Human Security and Gendered Insecurity," *Security Dialogue,* Vol. 35, No. 4, 2004, pp. 465–479.

Fraser, Arvonne S., "Becoming Human: The Origins and Development of Women's Human Rights," *Human Rights Quarterly,* Vol. 21, No. 4, November 1999, pp. 853–906.

Gadio, Columba Mar, and Cathy A. Rakowski, "Farmers Changing Roles in Thiedueme, Senegal: The Impact of Local and Global Factors on Three Generations of Women," *Gender and Society,* Vol. 13, No. 6, 1999, pp. 733–757.

Gall, Carlotta, "For British in an Afghan Province, Initial Gains Against the Taliban," *The New York Times,* August 5, 2007, p. 1.

Gender Action web site. As of November 5, 2007: http://www.genderaction.org/

Gender Disparities as a Challenge to Human Development, Afghanistan National Human Development Report, January 2004.

Grace, Jo, *Gender Roles in Agriculture: Case Studies of Five Villages in Northern Afghanistan,* Kabul: Afghanistan Research and Evaluation Unit, Case Studies Series, March 2004.

Grenblatt-Harrison, Andrea, Nora O'Connell, and Shanta Gyan-Bryant, "Strengthening Afghan Women's Civil Society to Secure Afghanistan's Future: An Analysis of New U.S. Assistance Programs," Washington, DC: Women's Edge Coalition, January 2005. As of December 13, 2007: http://www.womensedge.org/index. php?option=com_kb&Itemid=72&page=articles&articleid=12

Haidari, Ashraf, "Afghanistan's Parliamentary Election Results Confirm Stunning Gains for Women," October 28, 2005. As of November 5, 2007: http://www.eurasianet.org/departments/civilsociety/articles/eav102805b.shtml

Heyzer, Noeleen, "Women, War and Peace: Mobilizing for Security and Justice in the 21st Century," United Nations Development Fund for Women (UNIFEM), September 22, 2004. As of October 31, 2007: http://www.unifem.org/news_events/story_detail.php?StoryID=173

———, "Gender Peace and Disarmament, Disarmament Forum," *Women, Men Peace and Security*, Vol. 4, 2003. As of November 5, 2007: http://www.unidir.org/pdf/articles/pdf-art1993. pdf#search=%22gender%20peace%20and%20disarmament%22

Hill, Felicity, "Women's Contribution to Conflict Prevention, Early Warning and Disarmament," *Women, Peace and Security*, United Nations Disarmament Forum, Vol. 4, 2003.

Hill, Luke, "NATO to Quit Bosnia, Debates U.S. Proposals," *Jane's Defence Weekly*, Vol. 40, No. 23, December 10, 2003.

Human Rights Watch, "Lessons in Terror: Attacks on Education in Afghanistan," *Human Rights Watch*, New York, NY, 2006. As of October 2006: http://hrw.org

———, "Afghanistan: Analysis of New Cabinet," *Human Rights Watch*, Vol. 20, June 2002a.

———, "Q&A on Afghanistan's Loya Jirga Process," *Human Rights News*, April 15, 2002b. As of October 2006: http://hrw.org

———, "Afghanistan: Loya Jirga Off to Shaky Start," *Human Rights News*, 13 June 2000. As of October 2006: http://hrw.org

Human Rights Watch Afghanistan, "We Want to Live as Humans," *Repression of Women and Girls in Western Afghanistan*, Vol. 14, No. 11, December 2002.

Human Security Centre, "The Human Security Report 2005." As of November 5, 2007:
http://www.humansecurityreport.info/

Hunt, Swanee, "Let Women Rule," *Foreign Affairs*, May/June 2007.

Inayatullah, Attiya, "Ensuring Human Security for Women: Family Planning and Reproductive Health," *Clash or Consensus? Gender and Human Security in a Globalized World*, Bethesda, MD: Women's Learning Partnership. As of December 17, 2007:
http://www.learningpartnership.org/en/news/events/2003/clashorconsensus

Inglehart, Ronald, Pippa Norris, and Christian Welzel, "Gender Equality and Democracy," *Comparative Sociology*, Vol. 1, No. 3–4, 2002. As of November 5, 2007:
http://ksghome.harvard.edu/~pnorris/Acrobat/
Gender%20equality%20&%20democracy.
pdf#search=%22Gender%20Equality%20and%20Democracy%20pippa%22

"Initiative for Inclusive Security," Women Waging Peace Network. As of November 5, 2007:
http://www.womenwagingpeace.net/toolkit.asp

International Center for Research on Women, "After the Peace: Women in Post-Conflict Reconstruction," *Information Bulletin Series*, Washington, DC: International Center for Research on Women, November 1998. As of December 13, 2007:
http://www.icrw.org/docs/postconflictinfobulletin.pdf

International Crisis Group, "Afghanistan: Judicial Reform and Transitional Justice," *Asia Report No. 45*, January 28, 2003. As of October 31, 2007:
http://www.crisisweb.org

———, "The Loya Jirga: One Small Step Forward?" New York: International Crisis Group, Asia Briefing Paper, May 16, 2002.

International Development Research Center, *Annual Report*, Canada, 2004.

International Republican Institute, "Voter Education Planning Survey: Afghanistan, 2004 National Elections," in cooperation with the Asia Foundation, Kabul, 2004a.

———, "Afghanistan: Election Day Survey," Kabul, October 9, 2004b.

International Women's Democracy Center web site. As of November 5, 2007:
www.iwdc.org

Inter-Parliamentary Union, *Women in Politics 1945–2005*, Geneva, February 2005. As of November 5, 2007:
http://www.ipu.org/PDF/publications/wmn45-05_en.pdf

Iselin L. Danbolt, Nyaradzai Gumbonzvanda, and Kari Karame, "Toward Achieving the MDGs in Sudan: Centrality of Women's Leadership and Gender Equality," The Government of Norway and UNIFEM, 2005. As of November 5, 2007:
http://www.peacewomen.org/resources/Sudan/UNIFEM_MDGs_Sudan.pdf

"Islamic Feminism: Perils and Premises," *Middle East Women's Studies Review,* Vol. 16, No. 13, Fall 2001, p. 14.

Johnson, Nicola, "Evaluation of DFID Development Assistance Gender Equality and Women's Empowerment, Phase II Thematic Evaluation: Conflict and Post Conflict Reconstruction," Department for International Development, United Kingdom, March 2005.

Joint Electoral Management Body, "Statistics on Women and the Elections," Report, Kabul, Afghanistan, September 2005. As of November 5, 2007:
http://www.jemb.org/eng/Gender/stats_women_on_elections-eng.pdf

Jones, Seth G., Lee H. Hilborne, C. Ross Anthony, Lois M. Davis, Federico Girosi, Cheryl Benard, Rachel M. Swanger, Anita Datar Garten, Anga R. Timilsina, *Securing Health: Lessons from Nation-Building Missions,* Santa Monica, CA: RAND Corporation, MG-321-RC, 2006. As of November 4, 2007:
http://www.rand.org/pubs/monographs/MG321/

Joseph, Saud, "Gender Citizenship in the Middle East," in Saud Joseph (ed.), *Gender and Citizenship in the Middle East*, Syracuse, NY: Syracuse University Press, 2000.

———, "Gender and Citizenship in Middle Eastern States," *Middle East Report, No. 198, Gender and Citizenship in the Middle East,* January–March, 1996, pp. 4–10.

Joshi, Vijay, "Violence Against Women Rampant in Asia," Associated Press International, 2005.

Kai, Lt. Col. Janet, "Afghan Women Increasing Role in Army," *Defend America News,* November 17, 2005.

Kakar, Palwasha, *Fine-Tuning the NSP: Discussions of Problems and Solutions with Facilitating Partners*, Afghanistan Research and Evaluation Unit, November 2005. As of December 13, 2007:
http://www.cmi.no/pdf/?file=/afghanistan/doc/AREU%20Nov%2005%20Fine-tuning%20the%20NSP.pdf

Katzman, Kenneth, "Afghanistan: Elections, Constitution, and Government," CRS Report for Congress, Foreign Affairs, Defense, and Trade Division, The Library of Congress, Washington, DC, May 2006. As of November 5, 2007:
http://fpc.state.gov/documents/organization/67158.pdf

Kaufmann, Daniel, "Myths and Realities of Governance and Corruption," *Global Competitiveness Report*, Geneva: World Economic Forum, 2005–2006.

Kaufmann, Daniel, Aart Kraay, and Massimo Mastruzzi, *Governance Matters IV: Governance Indicators for 1996–2004*, Washington, DC: The World Bank, 2004.

Khong, Yuen Foong, "Human Security: A Shotgun Approach to Alleviating Human Misery?" *Global Governance*, Vol. 7, No. 3, September 2001.

King, Elizabeth, and Andrew Mason, "Engendering Development Through Gender Equality in Rights, Resources, and Voice," Washington, DC: The World Bank, A World Bank Policy Report, Vol. 1, 2001. As of November 5, 2007: http://www-wds.worldbank.org/external/default/WDSContentServer/IW3P/IB/2001/03/01/000094946_01020805393496/Rendered/PDF/multi_page.pdf

King, Gary, and Christopher Murray, "Rethinking Human Security," *Political Science Quarterly*, Vol. 116, No. 4, 2001–2002.

Kirk, Jackie, "Promoting a Gender-Just Peace: The Roles of Women Teachers in Peace Building and Reconstruction," in Caroline Sweetman (ed.), *Gender, Peacebuilding, and Reconstruction*, Oxford, UK: Oxfam Publishing, 2005. As of November 5, 2007: http://www.oxfam.org.uk/what_we_do/resources/downloads/gender_peacebuilding_and_reconstruction_kirk.pdf

Linking Complex Emergency Response and Transition Initiative (CERTI) web site. As of November 5, 2007: http://www.certi.org/themes/Peace_Building-Conflict.htm

Liotta, P. H., "Boomerang Effect: The Convergence of National and Human Security," *Security Dialogue*, Vol. 33, No. 4, 2002.

Lister, Sarah, "Moving Forward? Assessing Public Administration Reform in Afghanistan," Kabul: Afghanistan Research and Evaluation Unit, briefing paper, September 2006.

Maley, William (ed.), *Fundamentalism Reborn? Afghanistan and the Taliban*, New York: New York University Press, 2001.

Mani, Rama, *Ending Impunity and Building Justice in Afghanistan*, Kabul: Afghanistan Research and Evaluation Unit, 2003.

Manuel, Anja, and P. W. Singer, "A New Model Afghan Army," *Foreign Affairs*, Vol. 81, No. 4, July/August 2002.

Mao Tse-tung, *Selected Military Writings of Mao Tse-Tung*, Peking, China: Foreign Language Press, 1963.

Marshall, Donna Ramsey, *Women in War and Peace*, Washington, DC: United States Institute of Peace, Peace-works Series, No. 34, August 2000. As of November 5, 2007: http://www.usip.org/pubs/peaceworks/pwks34.pdf

McNerney, Michael J., "Stabilization and Reconstruction in Afghanistan: Are PRTs a Model or a Muddle?" *Parameters,* Vol. 35, No. 4, Winter 2005–2006.

Medica Mondiale, "Trapped by Tradition: Women and Girls in Detention in Kabul," Cologne, Germany. As of October 2006:
http://www.medicamondiale.org/download/doku_report/KabulHaftReport_e.pdf

———, *Violence Against Women in War: Handbook for Professionals Working with Traumatised Women*, Cologne, Germany. As of November 5, 2007:
http://www.medicamondiale.org/_en/bibliothek/eigene/handbuch/

———, *Lobbying and Defending Women's Rights*, Cologne, Germany, Projects, 2006.

———, *Legal Aid Program, Facts and Figures,* Cologne, Germany, Projects, 2004.

Miller, Laurel, and Robert Perito, *Establishing the Rule of Law in Afghanistan*, Washington, DC: United States Institute of Peace, Special Report No. 117, March 2004. As of November 5, 2007:
http://www.usip.org/pubs/specialreports/sr117.html

Moghadam, Valentine M., "Revolution, Religion, and Gender Politics: Iran and Afghanistan Compared," *Journal of Women's History,* Vol. 10, No. 4, Winter 1999.

Moghadam, Valerie, "Globalization and Women in the Middle East," *Middle East Women's Studies Review*, September 2002.

Naraghi-Anderlini, Sanam, *Women, Peace and Security: A Policy Audit: From the Beijing Platform for Action to UN Security Council Resolution 1325 and Beyond—Achievements and Emerging Challenges*, International Alert, June 2001. As of November 5, 2007:
http://www.international-alert.org/publications/106.php

Nassery, Homira, *Gender Disparities as a Challenge to Human Development*, United Nations, Human Development Report, New York: United Nations Press, January 2004.

National Solidarity Program, *NSP Operations Manual*, Version 3, January 15, 2006.

———, *NSP Weekly Report*, December 31, 2005a. As of December 13, 2007:
http://www.nspafghanistan.org

———, *NSP Monthly Report*, October 2005b. As of December 13, 2007:
http://www.nspafghanistan.org

———, *Third Quarter Report*, July–September 2005c. As of December 13, 2007:
http://www.nspafghanistan.org

———, *NSP Operations Manual*, October 13, 2004.

———, *Donors to the National Solidarity Program.* As of December 13, 2007:
http://www.nspafghanistan.org

Nojumi, Neamat, Dyan Mazurana, and Elizabeth Stites, *Afghanistan's System of Justice, Formal, Traditional and Customary*, Boston, MA: Tufts University, Feinstein International Famine Center, June 2004.

Osirim, Mary Johnson, "Carrying the Burdens of Adjustment and Globalization: Women and Microenterprise Development in Urban Zimbabwe," *International Sociology*, Vol. 18, No. 3, 2003, pp. 535–558.

Paris, Roland, *At War's End: Building Peace After Civil Conflict*, New York: Cambridge University Press, 2004.

———, "Human Security: Paradigm Shift or Hot Air?" *International Security*, Vol. 28, No. 2, Fall 2001.

PBS, Frontline, "Filling the Vacuum: The Bonn Conference," As of November 5, 2007:
http://www.pbs.org/wgbh/pages/frontline/shows/campaign/withus/cbonn.html

Pearson Peacekeeping Centre, *Challenges of Peace Operations: Into the 21st Century*, Report on the VII Seminar, Human Rights and Gender Issues in Peacekeeping, 2001.

Pyle, Jean, and Kathryn Ward, "Recasting Our Understanding of Gender and Work During Global Restructuring," *International Sociology*, Vol. 18, No. 3, 2003.

Quinones, Adriana, *Gender and Post Conflict Reconstruction: The World Bank Track Record*, Washington, DC: Heinrich Böll Foundation, 2004. As of November 5, 2007:
http://www.genderaction.org/images/Boell%20Brookings%20Gender-Conflict%20Report.pdf

RAND-MIPT Incident Database, through June 2006. As of November 5, 2007:
http://www.rand.org/ise/projects/terrorismdatabase/

Rashid, Ahmed, *Taliban: Militant Islam, Oil and Fundamentalism in Central Asia*, New Haven, CT: Yale University Press, 2000.

Rawi, Mariam, "Women in Afghanistan Today: Hopes, Achievements and Challenges," speech delivered at the University of South Australia, Adelaide, on April 2006. As of November 5, 2007:
http://www.rawa.org/rawi-speech.htm

Rehn, Elisabeth, and Ellen Johnson Sirleaf, *Women, War and Peace: The Independent Expert's Assessment on the Impact of Armed Conflict on Women and Women's Role in Peace Building*, New York: The United Nations, UNIFEM, 2002.

Rizzo, Helen, Katherine Meyer, and Ali Yousef, "Women's Political Rights: Islam, Status and Networks in Kuwait," *Sociology*, Vol. 36, No. 3, 2002.

Rome Statute of the International Criminal Court, The Hague, July 17, 1998. As of November 5, 2007:
http://www.un.org/law/icc/index.html

Rosemberg, Fúlvia, "Multilateral Organizations and Early Child Care and Education Policies for Developing Countries," *Gender and Society*, Vol. 17, No. 2, 2003, pp. 250–266.

Roy, Oliver, "Islam and Resistance in Afghanistan," 2nd ed., New York: Cambridge University Press, 1990.

Rummel, R. J., "Is Collective Violence Correlated with Social Pluralism?" *Journal of Peace Research*, Vol. 34, 1997, pp. 163–175.

Saleh, Amrullah, *Strategy of Insurgents and Terrorists in Afghanistan*, Kabul: National Directorate for Security, 2006.

Salish, Ain O., and Shirkat Gah, "Information Gathering Exercise on Forced Marriages," submission by Interights to the Home Office Working Group, England, March 2000.

Sassen, Saskia, "Governance Hotpots: Challenges We Must Confront in the Post-September 11 World," *Theory Culture, and Society*, Vol. 19, No 4, 2002, pp. 233–244.

Save the Children, "State of the World's Mothers 2007." As of December 13, 2007: http://www.savethechildren. org/campaigns/state-of-the-worlds-mothers-report/2007/

Schroen, Gary, *First In: An Insider's Account of How the CIA Spearheaded the War on Terror in Afghanistan*, New York: Ballantine Books, 2005.

Schutte, Stefan, *Searching for Security: Urban Livelihoods in Kabul*, Case Studies Series, Kabul: Afghanistan Research and Evaluation Unit, April 2006.

Sedra, Mark, *Challenging the Warlord Culture: Security Sector Reform in Post-Taliban Afghanistan*, Bonn, Germany: Bonn International Center for Conversion, 2002.

Shoemaker, Joylynne (ed.), with Camille Pampell Conaway, *Conflict Prevention and Transformation: Women's Vital Contributions*, Washington, DC: Inclusive Security: Women Waging Peace and the United Nations Foundation, conference report, February 23, 2005.

Sikosa, Tatjana, and Juliet Solomon, *Introducing Gender in Conflict and Conflict Prevention: Conceptual and Policy Implications*, New York: The United Nations Press, 2002.

Sorensen, Brigitte, *Women and Post Conflict Reconstruction: Issues and Sources*, United Nations Research Institute for Social Development, Programme for Strategic and International Security Studies, WSP Occasional Paper No. 3, New York: United Nations Press, June 1998.

Spees, Pam, "Gender Justice and Accountability in Peace Operations: Closing the Gaps," International Alert, Gender and Peace Building Program, February 2004. As of November 5, 2007:
http://www.international-alert.org/pdfs/gender_justice_accountability_peace_operations.pdf

Spink, Jeanine, *Situational Analysis Afghanistan Teacher Education Project, Teacher Education and Professional Development in Afghanistan*, Kabul: Afghanistan Research and Evaluation Unit, August 2004.

Steiner, Ambassador Steven, Acting Senior Coordinator for International Women's Issues, "Remarks to Democracy Assistance Dialogue Intergovernmental Conference on Women's Empowerment," Ankara, Turkey, May 23, 2006. As of Novembr 5, 2007:
http://www.state.gov/g/wi/66976.htm

Stoett, Peter, *Human and Global Security: An Exploration of Terms*, Toronto: University of Toronto Press, 1999.

Strickland, Richard, and Nata Duvvury, *Gender Equity and Peace Building: From Rhetoric to Reality: Finding the Way*, Washington, DC: International Center for Research on Women, 2003. As of November 5, 2007:
http://www.icrw.org/docs/gender_peace_report_0303.pdf#search=%22Gender%2
0Equity%20and%20Peacebuilding%3A%20from%20Rhetoric%20to%20Reality
%3A%20Finding%20the%20Way%22

Suhrke, Astri, "Human Security and the Interests of States," *Security Dialogue*, Vol. 30, No. 3, 1999, pp. 265–276.

Sultan, Masuda, *From Rhetoric to Reality: Afghan Women on the Agenda for Peace*, Women Waging Peace Policy Commission, Hunt Alternative Funds Publishing, February 2005.

Thomas, Caroline, and Peter Wilkin (eds.), *Globalisation, Human Security, and the African Experience*, Boulder, CO: Lynne Rienner, 1999.

Treverton, Gregory, and Seth G. Jones, *Measuring National Power*, Conference Proceedings, Santa Monica: CA, The RAND Corporation, 2005, RAND/CF-215. As of November 5, 2007:
http://www.rand.org/pubs/conf_proceedings/CF215/

United Nations, *Human Security Now: Commission on Human Security*, New York: United Nations Press, 2003, p. 4

_____ , *Discrimination Against Women and Girls in Afghanistan*, Report of the Secretary-General, Commission on the Status of Women, Forty-Sixth Session, March 4–15, 2002, Follow-up to the Fourth World Conference on Women, January 24, 2002.

_____ , *Road Map Towards the Implementation of the United Nations Millennium Declaration*, Report of the Secretary-General, Fifty-Sixth Session, United Nations

General Assembly, September 2001. As of November 5, 2007:
http://www.un.org/documents/ga/docs/56/a56326.pdf

———, *Mainstreaming a Gendered Perspective in Multidimensional Peace Operations*,
New York: United Nations Press, July 2000.

———, *Report of the UN Special Rapporteur on Violence Against Women: Mission to
Pakistan and Afghanistan*, New York: United Nations Press, 1999.

———, "UN Millennium Development Goals." As of November 4, 2007:
http://www.un.org/millenniumgoals/

United Nations Children's Fund, *The State of the World's Children 2004*, New
York: United Nations Press, 2004. As of November 4, 2007:
http://www.unicef.org/publications/files/Eng_text.pdf

———, "Afghanistan: Statistics." As of November 4, 2007:
http://www.unicef.org/infobycountry/afghanistan_afghanistan_statistics.html

United Nations Development Fund for Women, "UNIFEM Launches Database to
Track Violence Against Women in Afghanistan," New York: United Nations Press,
February 2006. As of November 4, 2007:
http://www.unifem.org/news_events/story_detail.php?StoryID=412

———, *Securing the Peace: Guiding the International Community Towards Women's
Effective Participation Throughout Peace Processes*, New York: United Nations Press,
October 2005.

———, "Gender Advocacy in Afghanistan," New York: United Nations Press,
2004a. As of May 2006:
http://www.undp.org.af/about_us/overview_undp_afg/dcse/prj_mowa.htm

———, *Getting It Right: Gender and Disarmament, Demobilization, and
Reintegration*, New York: United Nations Press, October 2004b. As of November
4, 2007:
www.smallarmssurvey.org/files/portal/spotlight/disarmament/disarm_pdf/2004_
UNIFEM.pdf

———, *UNIFEM Supporting Implementation of Security Council Resolution 1325*,
New York: United Nations Press, October 2004c. As of December 13, 2007:
http://www.womenwarpeace.org/1325_toolbox

———, *Not a Minute More: Ending Violence Against Women*, New York: United
Nations Press, 2003.

———, "Progress of the World's Women, Volume 1," New York: United Nations
Press, 2002, As of November 4, 2007:
http://www.unifem.org/resources/books_reports.
php?pageNum_rsResource=12&totalRows_rsResource=63

———, *Declaration on the Elimination of Violence Against Women*, New York: United Nations Press, 1994.

———, "The Elimination of Violence Against Women." As of November 4, 2007: http://afghanistan.unifem.org/programmes/GJ/EVAW/index.html

———, Portal for Women War and Peace, "Gender Profiles of the Conflict in Iraq." As of November 4, 2007: www.womenwarpeace.org/country_profiles

———, *Report on War and Women in Bosnia*, Women War and Peace Gender Profile Series. As of December 13, 2007: http://www.womenwarpeace.org/

United Nations Development Programme, *DDR: Reintegration Has Been Completed in Time and Within Costs*, Kabul: Afghan New Beginnings Programme, 2006.

———, *Human Development Report 2005,* New York: United Nations, 2005, p. 12.

———, *Gender Disparities as a Challenge to Human Development, Afghanistan National Human Development Report*, New York: United Nations Press, January 2004a.

———, *Security with a Human Face—Challenges and Responsibilities*, New York: United Nations Press, 2004b.

———, *Afghanistan National Human Development Report 2004, Security with a Human Face: Challenges and Responsibilities*, New York: United Nations Press, January 2004c.

———, *Gender Approaches in Conflict and Post-Conflict Situations*, New York: United Nations Press, 2001.

———, "Women's Political Participation and Good Governance: 21st Century Challenges," New York: United Nations Press, 2000.

———, *Pacific Human Development Report*, 1999. As of December 13, 2007: http://hdr.undp.org/reports/

———, *Human Development Report 1994,* New York: United Nations, 1994. As of December 13, 2007: http://hdr.undp.org/reports/

———, Human Development Report web site: http://hdr.undp.org/en/reports/

United Nations Division for The Advancement for Women, Department of Economic and Social Affairs, "Fourth World Conference on Women, Platform for Action," 1995. As of November 4, 2007: http://www.un.org/womenwatch/daw/beijing/platform/

United Nations, Economic and Social Commission for South Asia, Gender Statistics Programs. As of December 13, 2007:
http://www.unescap.org/esid/GAD/index.asp

United Nations Economic and Social Council, *Discrimination Against Women and Girls in Afghanistan*, Commission on the Status of Women, Forty-Sixth Session, March 2002.

——, *Follow Up to and Implementation of the Beijing Declaration: The Situation of Women and Girls in Afghanistan*, Commission on the Status of Women, Forty-Fifth Session, March 2001.

United Nations, Education, Scientific and Cultural Organization, "Education for All: Global Monitoring Report, 2005." As of November 4, 2007:
http://portal.unesco.org/education/en/ev.php-URL_ID=35874&URL_DO=DO_TOPIC&URL_SECTION=201.html

——, "Gender Parity in Secondary Education: Are We There Yet?" Institute for Statistics, No. 5, New York: United Nations Press, April 2005. As of December 13, 2007:
http://209.85.173.104/search?q=cache:V3Q3ht3H86IJ:www.uis.unesco.org/file_download.php%3FURL_ID%3D6094%26filename%3D11145162121UIS_factsheet_05_EN.pdf%26filetype%3Dapplication%252Fpdf%26filesize%3D145071%26name%3DUIS_factsheet_05_EN.pdf%26location%3Duser-S/+Gender+Parity+in+Secondary+Education:+Are+We+There+Yet%3F+Institute+for+Statistics&hl=en&ct=clnk&cd=2&gl=us

United Nations Human Settlements Programme, *Evaluation of UN-HABITAT: National Solidarity Program*, Ministry of Rural Rehabilitation and Development, July 2004.

United Nations Inter-Agency Network on Women and Gender Equity, "Information and Resources on Gender Equality and Empowerment of Women." As of November 4, 2007:
www.un.org/womenwatch

United Nations, Office for the Coordination of Humanitarian Affairs, "Afghanistan: Honour Killings on the Rise," *IRIN News*, September 2006. As of November 4, 2007:
http://www.irinnews.org/report.asp?ReportID=55574&SelectRegion=Asia&SelectCountry=AFGHANISTAN

——, "The Plight of the Afghan Woman: New Campaign to Encourage Girls into School," *IRIN News*, March 14, 2005. As of November 5, 2007:
http://www.afghan-web.com/woman/encouragegirlsschool.html

——, "Afghanistan: Community-Based National Solidarity Program Showing Results," Investor Relations Information Network (IRIN), March 10, 2004. As of November 5, 2007:
http://www.irinnews.org/report.asp?reportID=39980&SelectRegion=Central_Asia&SelectCountry=AFGHANISTAN

——, web site. As of November 5, 2007:
http://ochaonline.un.org

United Nations, Office of the Special Advisors of Gender Issues and Advancement of Women, Department of Economic and Social Affairs, web site. As of November 5, 2007:
http://www.un.org/womenwatch/osagi/

United Nations, Security Council, *Women, Peace, and Security: A Report by the Secretary General*, Report number S/2004/814, New York: United Nations Press, October 13, 2004. As of November 5, 2007:
http://www.peacewomen.org/resources/1325/SGReportWPS2004.pdf

——, *Report by the Secretary-General on Women, Peace, and Security*, Report number S/2002/1154, New York: United Nations Press, October 16, 2002. As of November 5, 2007:
http://www.peacewomen.org/un/UN1325/sgreport.pdf

United Nations, Security Council Resolution 1325. As of October 2005:
http://www.un.org/events/res_1325e.pdf

United Nations, Statistics Division, "Assessment of Countries' Capacity to Monitor MDG Indicators," 2006. As of October 25, 2007:
http://unstats.un.org/unsd/statcom/doc06/MDG-Tables.xls

——, Department of Economic and Social Affairs, "The World's Women 2005: Progress in Statistics," March 2005. As of November 4, 2007:
http://unstats.un.org/unsd/demographic/products/indwm/wwpub.htm

——, "Arab States: Regional Report," UNESCO Institute for Statistics, Montreal, Canada, 2002. As of November 4, 2007:
http://www.uis.unesco.org/file_download.php?URL_ID=5371&filename=10535763001Etats_arabesEN%28single%29.pdf&filetype=application%2Fpdf&filesize=629920&name=Etats_arabesEN%28single%29.pdf&location=user-S/

——, "Millennium Development Goals Indicators," As of December 13, 2007:
http://mdgs.un.org/unsd/mdg/Default.aspx

United Nations Transitional Assistance Group, *The Windhoek Declaration: The Namibia Plan of Action on Mainstreaming a Gender Perspective on Multi-dimensional Peace Support Operations*, Windhoek, Namibia, United Nations Press, May 2000. As of November 5, 2007:
http://www.un.org/womenwatch/osagi/wps/windhoek_declaration.pdf

United States Agency for International Development, *Afghanistan Rule of Law Project: Field Study of the Informal and Customary Justice in Afghanistan and Recommendations on Improving Access to Justice and Relations Between Formal Courts and Informal Bodies*, Washington, DC, April 30, 2005a.

———, *USAID/Afghanistan Strategic Plan: 2005–2010*, USAID, Washington, D.C., May 2005b, As of October 31, 2007:
http://www.usaid.gov/locations/asia_near_east/countries/afghanistan/ramp.html

United States Marine Corps, *After Action Report on Operations in Afghanistan*, Camp Lejeune, NC, August 2004.

University of Washington, Center for Women and Democracy web site. As of November 5, 2007:
www.womenanddemocracy.org

Unterhalter, Elaine, Chloe Challender, and Rajee Rajagopalan, "Measuring Gender Equality in Education," in Sheila Aikman and Elaine Unterhalter (eds.), *Beyond Access: Transforming Policy and Practice for Gender Equality in Education*, Oxford, UK: Oxfam Publishing, 2005. As of October 25, 2007:
http://publications.oxfam.org.uk/oxfam/add_info_010.asp

U.S. Army Training and Doctrine Command, *Observations and Lessons Learned: Task Force Devil, 1st Brigade Combat Team, 82nd Airborne Division*, Fort Leavenworth, KS, January 2004.

———, *Operation Enduring Freedom: Tactics, Techniques, and Procedures*, Fort Leavenworth, KS, December 2003.

U.S. Department of State, "Rice Says Afghanistan Set to Enter New Phase of Its Development," International Information Programs, January 30, 2006. As of October 31, 2007:
http://usinfo.state.gov/sa/Archive/2006/Jan/30-583095.html

———, "President Issues Directive to Improve the United States' Capacity to Manage Reconstruction and Stabilization Efforts," fact sheet on Presidential Directive, December 2005a. As of November 5, 2007:
http://www.state.gov/r/pa/prs/ps/2005/58067.htm

———, Office of the Coordinator for Reconstruction and Stabilization, "Post-Conflict Reconstruction: Essential Tasks," April 2005b. As of October 31, 2007:
http://www.state.gov/documents/organization/53464.pdf

———, Office of the Coordinator for Reconstruction and Stabilization. As of October 31, 2007:
http://www.state.gov/s/crs/

U.S. Department of State, Bureau of Intelligence and Research, "Complex Emergencies: Collecting Data, Managing Information, Seeking Knowledge," Conference Report, Humanitarian Information Unit, Workshop on System

Planning, New York, September 2003. As of November 5, 2007: www.smartindicators.org

Wafa, Saghar, and Baser Nader, *Field Notes and Observations of Gender and Local Level Decision-Making in Kabul City*, Kabul: Afghanistan Research and Evaluation Unit, February 2005

Wakefield, Shawna, *Field Notes and Observations of Gender and Local Level Decision Making in Robat-e Sangi, Heart Province*, Kabul: Afghanistan Research and Evaluation Unit, March 2005.

Wakefield, Shawna, with Brandy Bauer, *A Place at the Table: Afghan Women, Men and Decision-Making Authority*, Kabul: Afghanistan Research and Evaluation Unit, Briefing Paper, August 2005. As of December 13, 2007: http://unpan1.un.org/intradoc/groups/public/documents/APCITY/ UNPAN021667.pdf

Wali, Sima, "Testimony of Sima Wali," Institute for Afghan Studies, December 18, 2001. As of November 2007: http://institute-for-afghan-studies.org

Womankind Worldwide, "Taking Stock: Afghan Women and Girls Six Months On," July 2002. As of November 5, 2007: http://www.womankind.org.uk/takingstockdownloads.html

———, web site. As of November 5, 2007: http://www.womankind.org.uk/vision-and-mission.html

Women for Afghan Women, web site. As of November 5, 2007: http://www.womenforafghanwomen.org/

Women Living Under Muslim Laws, "Afghanistan: Urgent Need to Include Representatives of Women's Organizations and Civil Society Organizations in the Bonn Conference—November 2001." As of December 17, 2007: http://www.wluml.org/english/actionsfulltxt.shtml?cmd%5B156%5D=i-156-3182

Women's Environmental and Development Organization, *Beijing Betrayed, Women Worldwide Report That Governments Have Failed to Turn the Platform into Action, Executive Summary*, New York, March 3, 2005. As of November 2007: http://www.wedo.org/files/beijingbetrayed.htm

Women's International League for Peace and Freedom web site. As of November 5, 2007: www.Peacewomen.org

Woodrow Wilson International Center for Scholars, *More Than Victims: The Role of Women in Conflict Prevention*, Middle East Program, Washington, DC, 2004a, As of November 5, 2007: http://www.huntalternatives.org/download/59_more_than_victims_the_role_of_ women_in_conflict_prevention.pdf

———, *Political Transition in Afghanistan the State, Islam and Civil Society*, Asia program Special Report, No. 122, June 2004b.

Woodrow Wilson International Center for Scholars, with the RAND Corporation, *"Best Practices": Progressive Family Laws in Muslim Countries*, August 2005. As of November 5, 2007:
http://wilsoncenter.org/topics/pubs/English.pdf

Woodward, Bob, *Bush at War,* New York: Simon and Schuster, 2002.

World Bank, *Afghanistan: National Reconstruction and Poverty Reduction—the Role of Women in Afghanistan's Future*, Washington, DC: World Bank, March 2005.

———, Gender Statistics web site. As of November 2007:
http://genderstats.worldbank.org/home.asp

———, World Development Indicators Database. As of November 5, 2007:
www.worldbank.org/data/countrydata/countrydata.html

World Bank Group, "Gender and Law in Francophone Sub-Saharan Africa: The Role of the World Bank, Gender Responsive Institutional, Policy and Legal/Regulatory Frameworks," *Africa Regional Findings*, No. 155, March 2000.

World Health Organization, *Draft Guidelines on Gender-Relevant Indicators in Health Research*, 2004. As of November 5, 2007:
http://www.who.int/gender/documents/indicators/en/

———, *Gender and Women's Health: Gender Based Violence in Disasters*. As of November 5, 2007:
http://w3.whosea.org/en/Section13/Section390_8280.htm

Zakhilwal, Omar, *The Right to Choose in Afghanistan*, Institute for Afghan Studies, January 2002. As of October 2007:
http://institute-for-afghan-studies.org

Zuckerman, Elaine, and Marcia E. Greenberg, "The Gender Dimensions of Post-Conflict Reconstruction: An Analytical Framework for Policymakers," *Gender and Development, An Oxfam Journal*, Vol. 12, No. 3, 2004.